BÁNH MÌ

75 BÁNH MÌ RECIPES
for
Authentic & Delicious
Vietnamese Sandwiches

JACQUELINE PHAM

AVON, MASSACHUSETTS

DEDICATION

THIS BOOK IS dedicated to Má Mười, my loving aunt, who just happens to be an exceptional cook. *Má Mười* literally translates to "Aunt #10" in Vietnamese; she is the youngest sister of nine siblings. Her story is the stuff of the American dream. Má Mười came to the United States with almost nothing, but she somehow managed to get an excellent education and then went on to run a successful Vietnamese restaurant in San Jose, all while taking care of her husband and son.

Before opening her own restaurant, she traveled for months all over Asia, working as a sous-chef in the best restaurants, picking up many culinary secrets in order to make hers a success. She's a virtual encyclopedia of Vietnamese cuisine, and I've learned so much about my roots and culture, and Vietnamese cooking from her. When I was newly married, Má Mười pulled me aside and said *"vợ phải nấu ăn cho chồng mới là hạnh phúc,"* which approximately translates to "the best way to a man's heart (it roughly translates 'to achieve a blissful marriage') is through his stomach." If you've read my cookbooks or visited my website with any frequency, you'll know I took her suggestion to heart.

Thank you for everything, Má Mười. I hope this book makes you proud!

Published by Adams Media, a division of F+W Media, Inc.
57 Littlefield Street, Avon, MA 02322. U.S.A.
www.adamsmedia.com

ISBN 10: 1-4405-5077-8
ISBN 13: 978-1-4405-5077-5
eISBN 10: 1-4405-5078-6
eISBN 13: 978-1-4405-5078-2

Printed in China.

10 9 8 7 6 5 4 3 2 1

Always follow safety and common sense cooking protocol while using kitchen utensils, operating ovens and stoves, and handling uncooked food. If children are assisting in the preparation of any recipe, they should always be supervised by an adult.

Many of the designations used by manufacturers and sellers to distinguish their products are claimed as trademarks. Where those designations appear in this book and F+W Media was aware of a trademark claim, the designations have been printed with initial capital letters.

Photos by Jacqueline Pham.

This book is available at quantity discounts for bulk purchases.
For information, please call 1-800-289-0963.

ACKNOWLEDGMENTS

To Aria, my one-year-old daughter. You are my lucky charm. These cookbooks are in part my way of sharing with you our family's cultural heritage. When you're a little older, you'll get to know the dishes that made your great-grandmas the toast of Hyderabad and Saigon, respectively. There are lots of fun stories behind the recipes that I can't wait to share with you.

To Carole Florian, for being such an amazing friend and PhamFatale.com editor. Despite my crazy delays and schedule, you never fail to support me whenever I call. Our website, PhamFatale.com, wouldn't have reached the level of success it has without your help. You're always there for me through my ups and downs. It's a privilege to have met you and to have you in my life.

To my PhamFatale.com family. It's still so amazing to me that every month I can reach out to hundreds of thousands of foodies around the country and share my culinary creations. Even with 1,500 dishes photographed and published on the site, I would never have imagined in my wildest dreams that I'd be given the opportunity to publish one—let alone two—cookbooks. Thank you so much for your support and for letting me do what I love. I owe all of this to you!

To Ross, I'm so happy you contacted me last year! Thanks for making not only one, but two cookbook projects happen in less than a year. I'm humbled and honored that you considered me, and I hope you're as proud of the results as I am.

To Daddy and Chi Tine for the constant love and peace you have brought to my life. You are my rock. Thank you for always being there for me when I need you. Your love is my guide.

To Nathalie for being our Parisian guardian angel. After all you have done for us, I know how lucky Aria is to have you as her godmother. Every person has a few life-changing moments, and we are so fortunate that you were there to help us through the challenging ones. Please come and visit us in America soon.

To Cô Nho for keeping my little Aria so happy while I worked on the book. I don't tell you enough how much I appreciate your dedication and support.

To Sanah for being so patient while taking my headshot photos. You're such an exceptional and gifted person. Good luck with your college applications!

To Aelya, my workout buddy who got up early every morning with me and kept me on track to reach our goals. Not only have I shed the extra baby weight in a healthy way, but I also gained confidence. You're my partner in crime!

To Lulu, the love of my life. Thank you for your undying support. I love you more than you can imagine, and words cannot begin to express all that's in my heart. I've been blessed with many wonderful people in my life but your integrity and selflessness are a true inspiration. Thank you for showing me love and passion every day for the past twelve years and working so hard for our family. My love hasn't changed since the first day we met. *Je t'aime mon coeur.*

And finally, to the rest of my Girls. I've been so blessed to have the four of you in my life. I love you so much!

Each one of you has a special place in my heart; you have taught me valuable lessons that I cherish.

All my love,

Jackie

CONTENTS

INTRODUCTION

IMAGINE YOU'RE STANDING in the middle of a bakery. The intoxicating aromas of freshly baked baguettes and warm, flaky croissants fill the air. This scene could describe just about any Parisian *boulangerie* or its copycats across the world. But if you were to look a little closer, in this particular bakery you would also find spring rolls and eggrolls, Asian pearl drinks, and sandwiches filled with the most interesting ingredients.

That's the beauty of *bánh mì* shops. The French influence is undeniable, but at the same time these shops are distinct experiences unto themselves. Put another way, a *bánh mì* shop makes the foreign familiar and the exotic accessible. *Bánh mì* literally translates to "bread," so in addition to the French baguette, expect to find croissants, waffles, puff pastries, and other carbohydrate-rich delights. And like traditional boulangeries, *bánh mì* shops carry breakfast items, pastries, and drinks in addition to the wide selection of sandwiches. If you've always wanted to try Vietnamese food but felt too intimidated, a *bánh mì* sandwich filled with Vietnamese meatballs or chicken salad with pickled mango is a great place to start. Traditional Vietnamese cuisine places tremendous emphasis on a balance of colors, textures, and flavors. Dishes should appeal to all five senses, which means presentation carries quite a bit of weight. These sensibilities extend even to the less traditional *bánh mì* sandwiches. The bright tones of cilantro and thin strips of pickled carrots and daikon contrast with the earthy hues of the savory meats and bread. Condiments are not an afterthought in *bánh mì* sandwiches; rather, they play an integral role in creating the desired harmony. As you read through the book, you'll learn how to prepare a number of colorful, flavorful, and exotic condiments to pair with any number of savory meat and seafood recipes.

If you are lucky enough to live near a *bánh mì* shop, this book will take you on a tour of many of the culinary delights you can expect to find. And if you don't, you'll have all the tools and expertise you need to make a Vietnamese shredded pork–style sandwich, spring rolls, and an avocado smoothie for yourself. You'll even learn how to make a bubble milk tea for dessert. Now doesn't that sound a lot better than a turkey sub and diet soda from your neighborhood sandwich shop?

CHAPTER 1

BREAKFAST AND BRUNCH

Meat is an integral part of Vietnamese breakfast foods. Even if you prefer carbohydrates to protein for your morning meal, there are still some delectable treats for you to enjoy. Sesame Beignets (*Bánh Tiêu*) are very satisfying, out-of-the-ordinary pastries, and Coconut Waffles (*Bánh Kẹp Lá Dứa*) combine a traditional flavor of Vietnam (*pandan*) with a breakfast favorite. Deep-Fried Bread Sticks (*Bánh Giò Cháo Quảy*) are the perfect partner to a rich cup of Vietnamese Coffee (*Cà Phê Sữa*; see Chapter 7). For the bacon-and-eggs crowd, you'll find a meat-filled croissant and puff pastry pie, made popular because of the French influence on Vietnam. In this chapter, there's a breakfast treat for every taste.

CROISSANTS

Bánh Sừng Bò

YIELDS 25 CROISSANTS

What better way to start your discovery of a typical *bánh mì* shop than with the most envied pastry the French brought to Vietnam? *Bánh* croissants (also known as *bánh sừng bò*) are a little labor-intensive, but your effort will be worth it. The tricky part is folding the pastry dough to incorporate the layers of pure butter.

For the dough

¾ cup water
⅓ cup granulated sugar
1¾ tablespoons active dry yeast
4⅛ cups all-purpose flour
1 teaspoon vegetable oil
1½ teaspoons salt
¼–⅔ cup milk or water
2 tablespoons flour, for rolling dough
18 tablespoons unsalted butter

For the egg wash

1 egg
2 tablespoons milk

THE NIGHT BEFORE:

1. **For the leavening agent:** Warm ¾ cup water to between 105°F–120°F. Combine 1 tablespoon sugar, the active dry yeast, and the warm water. Once the sugar is dissolved, add ¼ cup flour. Mix to form a dough. Cover with a damp towel, place the bowl in a warm spot, and let rest 15 minutes.

2. **Making the dough:** Lightly oil the bowl of a stand mixer with a silicone brush. In a mixing bowl, combine the formed dough, the remaining all-purpose flour, the rest of the sugar, the salt, and ¼–⅔ cup milk (or water). Knead the dough at slow speed for 5 minutes until it becomes smooth. If it's too dry, add 1–4 tablespoons more milk. Score the top of the dough with a criss-cross incision. Cover with a towel, place the bowl in a warm spot, and let the yeast do its magic. You'll have a nice airy dough in about 90 minutes. Punch down the air bubbles in the dough. Seal it with plastic wrap and chill in the refrigerator for 30 minutes. Sprinkle a flat surface (a marble surface is preferred, so the dough remains cold) with 1 tablespoon flour. Dimple the dough with your fingers to shape it, then roll out the dough to about ¼" thickness and flatten it into 2 (8" × 8") squares with a rolling pin. Cover with plastic wrap and let rest in a warm spot overnight.

THE NEXT DAY:

3. **Preparing the butter:** Place the block of butter between 2 sheets of parchment paper or plastic wrap and roll the butter to flatten it into 2 (8" × 8") squares. Place the butter in the refrigerator for about 20–30 minutes. If you don't have time, place in the freezer for 10 minutes.

4. **Incorporating the butter:** Sprinkle a flat surface (preferably marble, so the dough remains cold during the folding process) with 1 tablespoon flour. Dimple the dough with your fingers again to shape the dough, place them side by side, then roll and flatten them together to make one big (16" × 8") rectangle with a rolling pin. Place the squares of butter on top of each other onto the center of the dough (the width of the butter rectangle should be the same as the dough rectangle). Fold the right side of the dough over the butter, then the left side toward the straight opposite edge of the dough. Seal the dough so the butter is totally enveloped. Make sure the folded edge is placed on your right hand side.

Roll the dough again lengthwise into a long rectangle (about 16" × 8"). Repeat the same folding procedure (make sure the folded edge is placed on your right hand side), then chill in the refrigerator for 30 minutes. Place the dough vertically in front of you, roll it again into a long rectangle, and fold again. Place in the refrigerator for another 30 minutes. Roll the dough again into a long rectangle, and fold in half. Place in the refrigerator for another 30 minutes. Roll the dough again and chill in the refrigerator again. Divide the dough in half lengthwise and chill in the refrigerator.

5. **Forming the croissants:** Cut the rectangle into triangles; the base of each triangle should be 4" and the height 8". (You should have 25 triangles total.) Make a small ¼" incision at the middle of the base of each triangle. Using the dough remnants, form 25 small balls of dough and set them aside. Place a little reserved piece of dough where each incision was made, then using both hands, start from the base of the triangle and gently roll and pull the dough until you reach the point of the triangle. Transfer to a baking pan lined with parchment paper, point side up. Gently pinch and flatten the ends, and push them close to each other, forming a crescent.

6. **For the egg wash:** Using a fork, beat the egg with 2 tablespoons milk. Lightly brush the egg wash over the croissants. Make sure to coat only the top and not the borders or the dough won't rise. Let sit at room temperature for 2 hours until the dough has expanded, then brush with the egg wash one more time. At this point, you can either freeze them for further use or bake them immediately.

7. **To bake:** Preheat the oven to 170°F. Fifteen minutes prior to baking, place a large bowl filled with 1 cup chilled water (for a higher humidity rate) in the center of the oven. Remove the bowl, increase the temperature to 375°F, and bake the croissants for 5 minutes. Turn the oven down to 350°F and bake for 10–15 minutes more, or until golden brown.

CROISSANTS: *Bánh Sừng Bò*

SESAME BEIGNETS

Bánh Tiêu

YIELDS 14 BEIGNETS

Bánh Tiêu is a hollow pastry made of sweet dough dotted with sesame seeds. The secrets for achieving good results are to use bread flour because of its higher level of gluten, which makes it bake better, and to add sugar so it doubles the volume while leavening the dough.

¾ cup water

1 teaspoon active dry yeast

⅓ cup granulated sugar, to taste

½ teaspoon baking ammonia (or baking powder)

2½ cups bread flour

½ teaspoon salt

¼ teaspoon five-spice powder (or vanilla extract, to taste)

1 teaspoon butter, melted

¼ cup white sesame seeds, plus more as needed

¾ cup peanut oil, plus more as needed

THE NIGHT BEFORE:

1. **For the leavening agent:** Warm ¼ cup of the water to between 105°F and 120°F. In a bowl, combine the warm water, active dry yeast, 1 tablespoon of the sugar, and the baking ammonia or powder. Once the sugar is dissolved, add ⅓ cup of the flour. Mix to form a dough. Cover with a towel, place the bowl in a warm spot, and let rest overnight.

THE NEXT DAY:

2. **For the sweet dough:** In a mixing bowl, combine the dough starter from the previous day, the remaining flour, remaining sugar, salt, five-spice powder (or vanilla extract), 1 teaspoon melted butter, and ½ cup water. Knead the dough using the dough hook of a stand mixer for 10 minutes until it becomes smooth. If it's too dry, add 1–2 tablespoons more water. Cover with a towel, place the bowl in a warm spot,

and then let the yeast do its magic. You'll have a nice, airy dough in about 3 hours.

3. **Forming the beignets:** Knead the dough manually one more time for 1 minute, then divide the dough into 14 portions. Dimple the dough with your fingers to shape it, then roll and flatten it into disks with a rolling pin. Place the sesame seeds onto a plate and roll the disks into the sesame seeds. Roll out the dough to about ¼" thickness. Cover with a towel and let it sit for another 30 minutes. Roll out the dough one more time, cover again, and let sit one last time for 10 minutes before frying.

4. **Preparing the oil:** Cover a cooling rack with paper towels and place the rack on top of a baking sheet (for easy clean-up of the drained oil). In a frying pan, heat the oil for about 2 minutes over high heat. Wait until the oil is slightly bubbly (not too hot, so the beignets will fry to a nice golden color). For optimum results when heating the frying oil, the thermometer should register 345°F–360°F. Test the oil by dropping a teaspoon of the batter into the hot oil. It should float but not swell.

5. **Frying the beignets:** Once the oil is hot, lower the heat to medium. Fry for 4–5 minutes until golden and crunchy, flipping each piece using a spider skimmer. The beignets will start to pop up and become puffy. Repeat the same procedure for the rest of the beignets, placing three beignets maximum per batch in the hot oil. Make sure the beignets don't touch each other while frying. Delicately lift each beignet, draining as much oil as possible, and transfer it to the cooling rack.

BAKING AMMONIA Baking ammonia is called *bột khai* in Vietnamese. It can be found online or in most Asian specialty markets. It will help the bread become very light and airy. It has a very strong ammonia smell that disappears once it's cooked. If you want to substitute baking powder, Rumford brand aluminum-free baking powder is an excellent choice. In general, Vietnamese cooking calls for single-action baking powder.

SESAME BEIGNETS: *Bánh Tiêu*

SUNNY-SIDE UP QUAIL EGG SANDWICH

Trứng Chim Cút Ốp La

YIELDS 1 SERVING

There is a lot of French influence in Vietnamese cuisine, which is readily apparent in this dish. *Ốp la* is the pidgin French term for *oeufs au plat* (the consonant sounds from the French term are swallowed), or sunny-side up eggs. *Trứng chim cút* (quail eggs) are a very common ingredient in Vietnamese cuisine. They're great not just for breakfast; *ốp la* also makes a tasty late-night snack.

4 quail eggs
2 tablespoons vegetable oil
1 green onion, finely chopped
½ teaspoon palm sugar, freshly grated
1 clove garlic, finely minced
1 red Thai chile pepper, thinly sliced (optional)
¼ teaspoon white pepper, freshly ground
2 teaspoons Fish Sauce (*Nước Mắm Chấm*; see Chapter 6) or Maggi Seasoning
1 individual baguette
¼ cup sliced cucumber
2 tablespoons *củ kiệu*, thinly sliced

1. **Preparing the eggs:** Crack the eggs into a small bowl, making sure not to break the yolks.

2. **Cooking the eggs:** Heat the oil in a small saucepan. Once the oil is hot, add the green onion and sprinkle with palm sugar. Cook for 10 seconds, stirring constantly. Add the garlic and stir-fry for 20 seconds until fragrant and golden. Immediately pour in the eggs and sprinkle with the red Thai chile slices (if using). Cover and let sit for 1 minute. Reduce the heat to the lowest setting. The egg yolks should still be slightly runny at this point. Top with a sprinkle of white pepper. Cover and let sit for 2 minutes until the white part of the eggs is just set and it becomes opaque.

3. **Sandwich assembly:** Drizzle with *nước mắm chấm* or Maggi Seasoning. Slide the eggs onto a plate and serve them sizzling with the baguette, cucumber, and *củ kiệu* on a separate plate. Dip the bread into the yolk to absorb the egg flavors, and pick up the eggs with more bread.

BACON, *CHẢ LỤA*, EGG, AND CHEESE CROISSANT

Bánh Mì Croissant Chả Lụa Pho Mát

YIELDS 1 SERVING

Here's a classic choice for a protein-filled breakfast. Start the morning with a hot croissant sandwich filled with a common combo: *chả lụa* (Vietnamese-style bologna sausage), bacon, *thịt nguội* (Vietnamese-style cold cuts), egg (*trứng gà*), and cheese (*pho mát*).

2 eggs, at room temperature

2 tablespoons milk

½ teaspoon black pepper, coarsely ground

1 strip bacon

1 clove garlic, peeled and crushed

1 tablespoon each green, red, and yellow bell pepper, diced

1 teaspoon jalapeño green pepper, chopped

1 tablespoon butter

¼ teaspoon salt

1 tablespoon cilantro, chopped, plus more for garnish

1 slice sharp Cheddar cheese

1 slice Vietnamese-Style Cold Cuts (*Thịt Nguội*; see Chapter 4)

1 slice *chả lụa* (Vegetarian Bologna Sausage (*Chả Lụa Chay*), Chapter 2; Chicken Bologna Sausage (*Chả Lụa Gà Chiên*), Chapter 3; or Steamed Ham Roll (*Chả Lụa Bì*), Chapter 4)

1 croissant

2 teaspoons Fish Sauce (*Nước Mắm Chấm*; see Chapter 6) or Maggi Seasoning

1. **Preparing the eggs:** In a bowl, lightly beat the eggs with milk using a fork. Do not over-beat; whisk until just combined. Add ¼ teaspoon black pepper.

2. **Cooking the bacon:** In a small nonstick pan, cook the bacon until it reaches the desired crispness. Remove from the pan and cut in half. Set aside the bacon, leaving the drippings in the pan.

3. **Making an omelet:** Using the same small pan, cook the garlic in the bacon drippings until slightly golden. Add the bell peppers and jalapeño pepper. Once they're fragrant, add butter. When the butter is hot and golden, immediately pour in the egg mixture. Sprinkle with salt. Allow mixture to sit for about 20 seconds. Using a small spatula (or chopsticks), lift the cooked edges to let the uncooked eggs slide underneath the omelet so they will cook evenly. Sprinkle with cilantro and ¼ teaspoon black pepper. Top with the cheese slice and sliced meats. Cover with a lid. Turn off the heat and let it sit for 2 minutes.

4. **Sandwich assembly:** Cut lengthwise into the croissant. Drizzle the inside of the croissant with *nước mắm chấm* or Maggi Seasoning. Fill the sandwich with the omelet, the *thịt nguội*, and the *chả lụa*. Top with the strips of bacon and garnish with extra cilantro.

CHẢ LỤA For this recipe you can use Vegetarian Bologna Sausage (*Chả Lụa Chay*), Chapter 2; Chicken Bologna Sausage (*Chả Lụa Gà Chiên*), Chapter 3; or Steamed Ham Roll (*Chả Lụa Bì*), Chapter 4. Regular ham or regular bologna could be an alternative if you don't have *chả lụa*.

MEAT PUFF PASTRY PIE

Bánh Patê Sô

Bánh Patê Sô is also known as *pâté chaud*. It's made of rounds of flaky puff pastry with a meat filling seasoned with Vietnamese flavors, which is very similar to *chả giò* (eggrolls); see Chapter 6.

½ pound pork, freshly ground

1½ teaspoons baking powder

¼ cup leeks (green part only), chopped

2 teaspoons granulated sugar

1 tablespoon freshly grated ginger

½ teaspoon salt

1 teaspoon black pepper, freshly ground

1 carrot, peeled and finely chopped

1 white onion, chopped

4 ounces water chestnuts, drained and chopped

½ cup wood ear mushrooms, thinly sliced

1 teaspoon mushroom seasoning salt (*bột nêm*), (or regular salt)

12 (5" × 5") squares frozen puff pastry, thawed

1 egg yolk

1 tablespoon water

½ cup vegetable oil (or any neutral oil), as needed (for frying)

1 tablespoon butter, melted

1. **Preparing the meat:** In a large bowl, combine the ground pork, baking powder, leeks, sugar, and ginger. Season with salt and pepper. Cover with plastic wrap and refrigerate for at least 2 hours.

2. **Making *patê sô* filling:** Add carrot, white onion, water chestnuts, and wood ear mushrooms to the pork mixture. Sprinkle with mushroom seasoning salt. Mix well. Refrigerate the mixture until you're ready to form the *patê sô*.

3. **Preparing the puff pastry:** Using 3" scalloped-edge cookie cutters (or the rim of a glass), form 12 pastry rounds.

4. **For the egg wash:** Using a fork, beat the egg yolk with 1 tablespoon of water.

5. **Pastry assembly:** Gently prick the dough with a fork. Hold a large puff pastry round in the palm of your hand. Brush a thin layer of the egg wash around the edges of the round. Spoon about 1½ tablespoons meat mixture in the center of the round. Seal the puff pastry by covering the meat with another puff pastry round. Firmly press on the edges of the round. Seal and crimp the edges using the back of a fork. Create 6 pastries. Reserve the filling remnants for appetizers. Line a baking sheet with a silicone mat or a sheet of parchment paper. Place the pastries onto the baking sheet. Chill in the refrigerator for about 15–20 minutes before baking. Preheat the oven to 350°F. Brush the tops of the pastries with the remaining egg wash. Let dry for 10 minutes and brush with a thin layer of butter. Bake for 20–25 minutes until the top is golden. Allow the pastries to cool for a few minutes before eating.

STRAW MUSHROOM AND TOFU SCRAMBLE

Tàu Hủ Xào Nấm Rơm

YIELDS 4 SERVINGS

This tofu dish simulates scrambled eggs. Turmeric powder gives the tofu a yellow hue. If you're health conscious, you might consider this recipe; it's really hard to tell the difference from real scrambled eggs.

1 (12-ounce) package firm tofu

1 tablespoon vegetable oil

2 cloves garlic, finely minced

1 cup canned straw mushrooms, drained and halved lengthwise

1 tablespoon freshly grated ginger

½ teaspoon turmeric powder

1 teaspoon salt

¼ teaspoon black pepper, freshly ground

2 teaspoons green onions, chopped

2 tablespoons butter

1. **Preparing the tofu:** Cut the tofu into ½" slices. Blanch the tofu for about 3–4 minutes in boiling salted water. Drain the liquid. Let the tofu cool for 15–20 minutes. Pull on a pair of disposable gloves and mash the boiled tofu with your hands. The tofu should resemble large-sized cottage cheese curds. Set the tofu aside.

2. **Assembly time:** In a nonstick pan, heat the oil. Add the minced garlic. Cook for 2 minutes until it's fragrant and slightly golden. Add the mushrooms, quickly stir-fry for 1 minute, then transfer to a plate. Add the grated ginger and cook for another minute. Add the mashed tofu (don't over-crowd the pan). Sprinkle with turmeric powder. Season with salt and pepper. Lower the heat to medium. Cook for about 6–8 minutes. Stir occasionally to prevent the tofu from sticking to the bottom of the pan. Lastly, add butter and return the mushrooms and garlic to the pan. Toss all the ingredients well and serve.

COCONUT WAFFLES

Bánh Kẹp Lá Dứa

YIELDS 8 WAFFLES

There is something about the warmth, the bright color, and the crispy texture of Vietnamese waffles that is beyond compare. Maybe it's the fragrant steam coming off the waffle iron that's so enticing. *Bánh Kẹp Lá Dứa* are similar to Western waffles, but with an Asian touch: They're made with coconut milk, rice flour, and pandan extract.

1 cup all-purpose flour

½ cup rice flour

½ plus ¼ teaspoon salt, divided use

1½ teaspoons baking powder

½ teaspoon baking soda

3 tablespoons unsalted butter

1 (13.5-ounce) can coconut milk

2 large eggs, at room temperature

10 tablespoons granulated sugar

¾ teaspoon pandan extract

2 tablespoons water

3 tablespoons unsalted butter, melted

1. **Sifting the dry ingredients:** Preheat the waffle iron. In a bowl, combine the flours, ½ teaspoon salt, baking powder, and baking soda. Sift all the dry ingredients together into another bowl.

2. **Preparing the waffle batter:** In a small saucepan, melt the butter into ⅓ cup of the coconut milk over very low heat. Remove from the heat as soon as the butter is melted. Separate the eggs into two bowls, one for the yolks and one for the whites. Add 4 tablespoons of the sugar to the egg yolks and beat with an electric mixer until the mixture is thickened and pale yellow. Add pandan extract and stir until the color is uniform. Slowly add the flour mixture and the remaining 1⅓ cups of the coconut milk to the egg yolks, alternating between the dry and wet ingredients in 3 stages

until all the ingredients are used. Using a spatula, mix until the batter is well incorporated. Thin the batter with 2 tablespoons of water. Stir until combined.

3. **Finalize the batter:** Make sure your hand-held or stand mixer blades are thoroughly washed. Add ¼ teaspoon salt to the egg whites and beat just until stiff peaks form when you lift the mixer blades (don't overmix or it will become grainy). Add the remaining 6 tablespoons sugar. Spoon ⅓ of the egg white mixture into the waffle mixture, then gently stir everything together to soften the batter. Spoon in the rest of the egg whites and gently fold them in to make an airy batter.

4. **Bake the waffles:** Brush the plates of the waffle maker with melted butter for every waffle. Pour a scant ½ cup of waffle batter into the center of the waffle maker. Do not overfill or it will spill out the sides. Close the lid and cook the waffle for about 4 minutes until lightly brown. Repeat with remaining batter. Cut each waffle into 4 pieces to serve.

PANDAN You could color the waffles with ½ bunch fresh or frozen pandan leaves if you don't want to use artificial green food coloring (there is green food coloring in store-bought pandan extract). Simply add the pandan leaves tied in a knot to warm coconut milk. Cook over low heat for 5 minutes. Cover, turn off the heat, and let brew until the milk cools to room temperature. The pandan leaves will give the milk a nice fragrance and a faint pale green color. Remove and discard the leaves. (Note: Make sure to heat the milk over low heat; overheated milk might seize if not handled properly due to its fat content. Coconut milk is very unstable and may separate if the temperatures are too high—no more than 180°F.)

COCONUT WAFFLES: *Bánh Kẹp Lá Dứa*

RED BEAN SESAME BALLS

Bánh Cam Đậu Đỏ

YIELDS 22 BALLS

Bánh cam balls are simply named after their natural orange color once they're deep-fried. The authentic version calls for mung bean filling, but red beans are so much more satisfying. The sesame-covered, crisp, sweet fried balls ooze with warm red bean filling. Pair them with a hot cup of green tea (*trà xanh*) or Vietnamese Coffee (*Cà Phê Sữa*, see Chapter 7), and you'll have the most delightful breakfast.

½ cup dried azuki beans (*đậu đỏ*)

2½ cups plus 1¾ cups water, divided use

8 tablespoons granulated sugar

2 teaspoons vegetable oil

4 ounces freshly grated coconut (or store-bought unsweetened shredded coconut)

½ cup rock sugar, to taste

½ cup Chinese brown sugar (*đường thẻ*) (or regular brown sugar)

2 red potatoes

4½ cups glutinous rice flour (*bột gạo nếp*)

¼ cup jasmine rice flour

2 tablespoons baking powder

½ teaspoon salt

1 (8-ounce) jar sesame seeds

1 quart vegetable oil, as needed

THE DAY BEFORE:

1. **For the red beans:** Wash and rinse the azuki beans thoroughly in several water baths (about three times), discarding any floating or odd-shaped beans. Soak overnight in enough cold water to completely cover the beans.

THE NEXT DAY:

2. **Preparing the beans:** Rinse and drain the beans. Fill a saucepan with 2½ cups water and bring to a boil. (Count one part uncooked red beans to 4–5 parts water.) Add the azuki beans and cook for about 1–2 hours, until softened. Stir every now and then so the beans don't stick to the bottom of the saucepan. When the beans are completely cooked, they will feel soft when gently pressed between your thumb and index finger. If necessary, add ½ cup water and extend the cooking time by 30 minutes or until the beans are softened. Turn off the heat. Drain off any remaining liquid. Transfer the beans to a food processor and pulse until a coarse paste forms.

3. **Sweetening the beans:** In a nonstick saucepan, melt 8 tablespoons granulated sugar without any water over high heat. It's important to watch the sugar carefully; as soon as the sugar at the edges of the pan starts caramelizing, immediately lower the heat to medium-low. Gently move the saucepan in circles as soon as the sugar is melted (without getting too dark). Add the bean mixture to the sugar and mix well.

4. **For the bean filling:** Heat 2 teaspoons oil in a nonstick pan, add the red bean mixture, and stir-fry until the paste is thickened and dry. Let cool to room temperature. Mix in the grated coconut and divide into 20 equal portions.

5. **For the syrup:** Place ½ cup each rock sugar and Chinese brown sugar in a saucepan. Add 1¾ cups water. Give it a quick stir and bring to a boil, then let simmer until the sugar is completely dissolved. Remove from the stove and cool to room temperature.

6. **Boiling the potatoes:** Brush and wash the potatoes. Peel and cut them into quarters. Place them in a large pot and add cold water until the potatoes are barely covered. Bring to a boil and reduce the heat to medium-high. Cook for about 30 minutes, until tender. Drain the potatoes

thoroughly (without rinsing) and let them cool a little. Once the potatoes are cool enough to handle and have dried thoroughly, pass them through a potato ricer. Add the cooled syrup to the riced potatoes and mix well.

7. **Making the dough:** Add rice flours, baking powder, and salt to the warm potato mixture. When the mixture becomes almost like moist modeling clay, form 20 small dough balls. If the dough is too dry to stretch, gradually add up to 5 tablespoons cold water. Line a flat surface with a sheet of parchment paper or plastic wrap. Sprinkle with a thin layer of rice flour and flatten the dough into about 3½"-diameter disks; even out to about ½" thick.

8. **Forming the dough balls:** Place a portion of the red bean mixture in the center of a dough disk and delicately bring up the edges of the dough to cover the red beans, forming a larger ball and leaving no filling visible. The dough should be pinched at the top to seal the edges, and then the ball rolled between the hands to smooth it before rolling it in the sesame seeds. Place sesame seeds in a deep plate and transfer the dough ball to the plate. Roll until well coated. Roll the ball between your hands to ensure the sesame seeds adhere to the dough ball. Repeat with remaining dough and bean mixture. Let the dough balls set for 1 hour.

9. **Frying the dough balls:** Layer a cooling rack lined with paper towels on top of a baking sheet (for easy cleanup of the drained oil). In a large Dutch oven (or any regular deep-fryer), heat the oil for about 2 minutes over high heat. There should be at least 4" of oil (the balls should be submerged in oil when they fry). Wait until the oil is slightly bubbly (not too hot, to ensure a golden color after frying). For optimum results when heating the frying oil, the thermometer should register 325°F–350°F. Test the oil by dropping a teaspoon of dough into the hot oil. It should float but not swell. Place the dough balls one at a time in the hot oil. Fry in batches; you want to make sure they're entirely covered in the hot oil. Deep fry for 6–7 minutes per batch until golden, rotating them frequently. Remove each ball with chopsticks or a slotted spoon, draining as much oil as possible, and transfer the balls to the cooling rack. Let them cool for 15 minutes. When ready to eat, lightly flatten the balls and the warm red bean filling will ooze out.

RICE FLOUR Using freshly ground rice flour produces a crispier result. Simply use a combination of jasmine and sweet round rice (also known as glutinous sticky rice) and grind the grains into a fine powder using a food processor or spice grinder. You can find these particular types of rice in any Asian market.

RED BEAN SESAME BALLS: *Bánh Cam Đậu Đỏ*

DEEP-FRIED BREAD STICKS

Bánh Giò Cháo Quẩy

YIELDS 12 PIECES

Bánh Giò Cháo Quẩy is mostly known as the bread that you dip in *cháo* (warm congee porridge). In addition, it makes an excellent pairing with *cà phê sữa nóng* (warm coffee with sweetened, condensed milk) in the morning.

1¼ cups water, divided use

2 teaspoons granulated sugar

½ teaspoon baking ammonia (or baking powder)

½ teaspoon baking soda

½ teaspoon potassium alum (*phèn chua*), optional

1½ cups bread flour

¾ teaspoon salt

1½ cups peanut oil, plus more as needed

1. **For the leavening agent:** Warm ¼ cup water to between 105°F–120°F. Combine sugar, baking ammonia (or baking powder), baking soda, and alum (if using), and mix into the warm water. Once the sugar is dissolved, add ⅓ cup flour. Mix to form a dough. Cover with a towel, place the bowl in a warm spot, and let rest for 1 hour.

2. **For the sweet dough:** In a mixing bowl, combine the leavening agent, the remaining flour, salt, and 1 cup water. Knead the dough until it becomes smooth. If it's too dry, gradually add up to ¼ cup more water, 1 tablespoon at a time. If it's too sticky, sprinkle in a bit of flour (up to 2 tablespoons). Seal with plastic wrap, place the bowl in a warm spot, then let the yeast do its magic for 1 hour.

3. **Forming the bread sticks:** Shape the dough. Divide the dough in half. Brush a flat surface with a very thin layer of oil. Roll the dough and flatten it into 4"-long strips with a rolling pin. Then, roll out the 2 dough strips to about ¼" thickness. Using kitchen shears, snip the strips into 24 (½" ×

2½") rectangles. Cover with a sheet of greased plastic wrap. Let sit for another 30 minutes before frying.

4. **Preparing the oil:** Cover a cooling rack with paper towels and place the rack on a baking sheet (for easy cleanup of the drained oil). In a frying pan, heat at least 1" of oil over high heat for about 2 minutes, to a temperature of 345°F–360°F. Wait until the oil is slightly bubbly (not too hot, for a nice golden color after frying). Test the oil by dropping a pea-sized piece of dough into the hot oil. It should float immediately.

5. **Frying the bread sticks:** Brush the top of the strips with water. Pick up 2 strips and press the wet sides together. Then, press the back of a butter knife horizontally into the center of the strips, forming a small, deep cavity that creates the characteristic shape of a *giò cháo quẩy*. Doing this also helps the two strips adhere to each other. Pull and stretch each formed piece into a 5"–6" long strip. Once the oil is hot, lower the heat to medium. Fry for 4–5 minutes until golden and crunchy, flipping each piece with a spider skimmer. The bread sticks will start to pop and become puffy. Delicately lift the fried bread sticks, draining as much oil as possible, and transfer them to the cooling rack.

POTASSIUM ALUM   Potassium alum gives a more airy texture to the bread sticks and helps increase the volume. You'll find it in the baking products aisle of most supermarkets.

VIETNAMESE BAGUETTE

Bánh Mì Baguette

YIELDS 10 BAGUETTES

The *bánh mì* sandwich can be made with any kind of long, thin loaf of bread. But if you're reaching for the most authentic version, you might want to try to make your sandwich with a crusty, hand-made Vietnamese-style baguette. The difference is they're made with rice flour. Count about ⅓ rice flour to ⅔ all-purpose flour. This bread is lighter, with a more crackly crust than a French baguette, because rice flour doesn't contain gluten and doesn't absorb water as quickly as all-purpose flour.

2 cups water, divided use

1 (¼-ounce) package active dry yeast, or ½ ounce fresh yeast (if available)

1 teaspoon diastatic malt powder (optional)

1 tablespoon barley malt syrup or honey (optional)

2 teaspoons baking ammonia (or baking powder)

1¾ cups rice flour

3¼ cups all-purpose flour

2 teaspoons salt

THE NIGHT BEFORE:

1. **For the leavening agent:** Warm ¼ cup water to reach between 105°F–120°F. In a bowl, combine the warm water, active dry yeast, 1 teaspoon of the diastatic malt powder (if using), 1 tablespoon of the malt syrup or honey (if using), and the baking ammonia or powder. Once the syrup is dissolved, add the rice flour, 1 cup of the all-purpose flour, and ¾ cup water. Mix to form a dough. Cover with a towel, place the bowl in a warm spot, and let rest overnight.

THE NEXT DAY:

2. **For the baguette dough:** In a mixing bowl, combine the dough starter from the previous day, the remaining all-purpose flour, salt, and 1 cup water. Knead the dough using the dough hook of a stand mixer for 10 minutes until it becomes smooth. If it's too dry, add 1–2 tablespoons more water. At this point, the dough should be stretchable to the point it could be almost paper thin at its thinnest stage. Cover with a towel, place the bowl in a warm spot, and then let the yeast do its magic. You'll have a nice, airy dough in about 3 hours.

3. **Forming the baguettes:** Knead the dough manually one more time for 1 minute, then divide the dough into 10 (4¼-ounce) portions. Slap, roll, and fold each dough portion against a flat surface and form mini 5" oval-shape baguettes. Place them into a silicone French bread pan (if available) or regular baking pan. Cover with a towel and let sit for another 30 minutes in a warm spot. Using a very sharp razor blade, score one long incision along the length of the bread in a 45° angle (traditional, authentic Vietnamese baguettes are slashed only once). Proof the baguettes one last time for 15 minutes before baking.

4. **Baking time:** 15 minutes prior to baking, place a baking dish filled with 1 cup chilled water (for a higher humidity rate) in the center of the oven. Preheat the oven to 475°F. Once the temperature is reached, place cold water in a spray bottle, then spray the wall of the oven. Immediately place the proofed baguettes in the oven, preferably on convection mode. Reduce the temperature to 425°F and bake for 10 minutes, then turn the oven down to 375°F and bake for 10–15 more minutes or until golden brown. Remove the baguettes from the oven and let cool for 10 minutes. Immediately prepare a *bánh mì* sandwich or lightly toast the bread prior to serving it.

SERVING SUGGESTION If the bread isn't eaten the same day, it's preferable to freeze it for future use. Because of its light texture and crackly crust, it's recommended to cut lengthwise into the baguette, then lightly toast the bread prior to filling the sandwich.

CHAPTER 2

VEGETARIAN SANDWICHES

Because of Buddhist teachings against the consumption of meat, Vietnamese cooking has a fair share of vegetarian "mock meat" dishes. Savory vegetarian dishes are often made with flavorful tofu and are prepared in a manner to imitate meat. In this chapter you'll find recipes for Vegetarian Bologna Sausage (*Chả Lụa Chay*), Seaweed Tofu (*Cá Chiên Chay*), Wheat Gluten Stir Fry (*Mì Căn Xào Nấm Bào Ngư*), and a favorite among vegetarians, Vegetarian Larb (*Bì Chay*), which is an explosion of flavors consisting of shredded fried tofu, thin crisp noodles, fried potato matchsticks, and more.

The recipes in this chapter are for typical vegetarian *bánh mì* fillings, ones you would find in a *bánh mì* shop. In general, use 1 small authentic Vietnamese baguette per serving, or ⅓ of a larger French baguette. (Try making your own! See the Vietnamese Baguette: *Bánh Mì Baguette* recipe in Chapter 1.) For each recipe, the final step includes sandwich assembly instructions. You can choose to use the suggested ingredients, or mix and match your favorite flavors to taste. The listed ingredients are a general guide, and you can customize your sandwiches for a unique *bánh mì* experience every time.

VEGETARIAN LARB

Bì Chay

YIELDS 8 SERVINGS

This sandwich is a vegetarian favorite. It's a play on *bì* (shredded pork), with pan-fried, shredded tofu taking the place of the meat. It's the perfect combination of sweet, sour, spicy, and savory flavors. Leftover filling can be stored in the freezer for future use.

1¼ cups jasmine rice flour or *thinh* (see sidebar)

1¼ cups vegetable oil (or any neutral oil), as needed

2 yellow onions, sliced

1 (2-ounce) package dried bean thread noodles

2 (12-ounce) packages firm tofu

1 large jicama

1 shallot, thinly sliced

2 carrots, peeled and shredded into 5"-long thick strips

1 teaspoon salt

1 teaspoon freshly cracked black pepper

1 pound taro root

2 sweet potatoes

4 Yukon Gold potatoes

1 tablespoon mushroom seasoning salt (*bột nêm*), (or regular salt)

1¼ tablespoons cane sugar (or granulated sugar)

¼ teaspoon red chile powder

1. **For the dry-roasted rice powder:** Dry-roast the jasmine rice in a large pan (14" diameter) on the stove. Stir the rice using chopsticks until the grains turn a rich brown color (about 5–7 minutes over high heat). Let cool. Grind the grains into a fine powder using a food processor or spice grinder.

2. **Frying the onions:** In a large pan, heat ¼ cup of oil. Once the oil is hot, add the onions and fry for 6–8 minutes until golden brown, stirring occasionally to prevent them from burning. Transfer to a plate lined with paper towels, leaving as much oil as possible in the pan.

3. **For the bean thread noodles:** Place the whole package of dried bean thread noodles in a bowl. Cut and discard the little threads. Add enough cold water to cover the noodles. Soak the noodles for 30 minutes, then drain. Chop into 1" pieces. The texture should be soft but not soggy.

4. **For the tofu:** Drain any liquid from the tofu. Pat dry with a paper towel. Slice the tofu into ½"-thick pieces. Add 2 tablespoons oil to the same pan used for the onions and reheat the oil. Fry the tofu slices for 3 minutes until lightly golden and transfer to a plate. Once the tofu is cool enough to handle, cut into very thin strips.

5. **For the jicama:** Peel and slice horizontally into ½"-thick pieces. In the same large pan, add about 2 tablespoons oil and fry the jicama slices until golden brown. Transfer to a plate. Once they're cool enough to handle, cut the pieces into very thin strips.

6. **For the carrots:** In the same pan, heat 2 tablespoons oil. Add the shallot and cook until golden. Add the carrots and drizzle with 2–3 tablespoons water. Stir-fry until softened. Season with salt and pepper. Transfer to a plate.

7. **For the soaked noodles, taro, and potatoes:** Peel and shred the taro root using a mandoline. Place in a large bowl. Fill the bowl with ice water (it should barely cover the taro root). Let sit for about 15 minutes, then drain all the liquid. Pat dry. Repeat the same procedure with the sweet and Yukon Gold potatoes. Add about 2 more tablespoons of oil to the same large pan used for the carrots. Sprinkle 4–5 tablespoons noodles (working in several batches) evenly into the pan. Do not stir. Wait for at least 2 minutes until one side is crisp but not golden. Transfer to a plate lined with

paper towels. In the same pan, add more oil (2 tablespoons at a time, as needed, so they don't stick to the bottom of the pan) and pan-fry the taro for 2–3 minutes until crisp and golden. Flip the taro using chopsticks. Continue until all the taro is fried; repeat the same procedure with the potatoes. Add more oil if necessary. When the taro and potatoes are fried and golden, transfer to a platter lined with paper towels. As soon as all the oil is drained, transfer the taro and potatoes to a large bowl.

8. **Making *bi chay*:** In another large mixing bowl, combine the jicama, fried noodles, and 2–3 tablespoons toasted rice powder. Toss until combined. Add the fried taro, potatoes, and tofu. Season with mushroom seasoning salt. Sprinkle with sugar. Adjust seasoning with chile powder, and salt and black pepper to taste. Toss well, then sprinkle with 1–2 tablespoons rice powder. Add the carrots and fried onions. Mix well.

9. **Sandwich assembly:** Use 1 baguette per serving. Cut lengthwise into the baguette and remove some of the crumb. Drizzle the inside of the baguette with Vegetarian Dipping Sauce (*Nước Chấm Chay*; see Chapter 6) or Maggi Seasoning. Spread a thin layer of softened butter on both sides of the bread. Fill the sandwich with *bì chay*, sliced cucumbers, and Pickled Vietnamese Cabbage (*Dưa Muối*; see Chapter 6). Garnish with 2 sprigs of cilantro. Close the sandwich tightly.

THINH Dry-roasted rice powder is called *thinh* in Vietnamese. You can buy ready-made *thinh* in Asian stores, but grinding your own makes a more fragrant, toasty-scented *bì*. You can use it for *bì* (shredded meat with *thinh*), or grilled lemon grass beef with *thinh*, served with *cơm tấm* (jasmine broken rice). You can also toss the rice powder in salad; it absorbs some of the moisture and helps keep the salad dry and crisp.

VEGETARIAN BOLOGNA SAUSAGE

Chả Lụa Chay

YIELDS 6 SERVINGS

If you're craving a sandwich piled high with luncheon meat but want to eat a healthy version, try making this vegetarian sausage. Tofu skin is tightly packed, rolled in fresh banana leaves, and steamed until firm. The result looks so similar to bologna sausage, and is so tasty, you could fool anyone.

1 teaspoon salt

16 ounces frozen rolled tofu skin, thawed

1 tablespoon vegetable oil, plus more as needed

1 (2") piece leek (white part only), finely chopped

3 tablespoons wood ear mushrooms (nấm mèo), sliced

1 teaspoon mushroom seasoning salt (bột nêm) (or regular salt)

2 teaspoons sugar

1 teaspoon wheat gluten (optional)

1 tablespoon soy sauce

1 teaspoon white pepper, freshly ground

1 teaspoon whole black peppercorns

1 teaspoon sesame oil

4 (10" × 10") frozen banana leaves, thawed

1. **Preparing the tofu skin:** Fill a large pot with water halfway. Bring to a boil. Add salt and enough cold water so the water becomes lukewarm. Add tofu skin and soak for 4–5 minutes. Drain and let cool for 15 minutes. Pat dry with a towel, removing as much moisture as possible.

2. **Cooking the tofu skin:** In a large pan, heat 1 tablespoon vegetable oil. Once the oil is hot, add chopped leek and wood ear mushrooms and cook until fragrant but not browned. Add the tofu skin, mushroom seasoning salt, and sugar. Stir-fry for 1 minute, sprinkle with wheat gluten (if using), and add soy sauce. Stir-fry for 10 minutes until the liquid evaporates completely. Add ground white pepper, whole peppercorns, and sesame oil. Mix well. Let cool for 1 hour before wrapping.

3. **Preparing the banana leaves:** Using a towel moistened in hot water, clean the leaves to soften them and to prevent tearing while rolling. Gently dry the damp leaves with a cloth.

4. **Forming the sausage:** Place a large piece of plastic wrap on a flat surface. Top with 2 sheets of banana leaves, forming a long sheet, and layer one over the other by about 3"–4". Make sure the veins of the leaves are placed horizontally. Line the second layers in the same manner, but place the veins of leaves vertically, on top of the horizontal leaves. Brush the leaves with a thin layer of oil. Wet your hands with warm water and spread handfuls of the tofu skin mixture in the center of the leaves. Gather the top part of the leaves, and fold 3 times until you reach the center where the tofu skin is placed. Gather the bottom part of the leaves, and fold 3 times until you reach the center. Tightly and slowly roll the leaves so the mixture forms a cylinder shape, and the folded parts overlap. Press gently with both hands for about 10 seconds, to ensure the sausage becomes firm. Secure and tie the roll in the center with a small piece of string. Roughly fold one end of the cylinder and let it sit on its base. Even out and trim the top end with kitchen shears. Gently press the tofu skin mixture so it's tightly packed. Fold down the top flaps and flatten them against the sausage. Make sure it's secured tightly; the sausage might be a bit on the thin side, but it will expand when cooked. Fold in the gathered opposite wings and flip to the opposite end. Repeat the same trimming and folding procedure on the other end to seal the sausage. Secure and tie the roll by sliding a long

piece of string underneath the sausage lengthwise to seal both ends. Loop the string through the widthwise knot to secure. Make 3 tight knots, at equal distance, around the width of the sausage to secure. Trim the excess strings.

5. **Steaming the sausage:** Pour water in the bottom of a steamer to a depth of at least 3". Place the rack in the steamer. Bring the water to a boil, then lower the heat to medium-high. Place the roll in the steamer; cover and steam for about 30–40 minutes. The roll should be soft and tender but still firm. Remove from the steamer. Let cool a little. Chill in the refrigerator for at least 2 hours. Remove and discard the strings. Transfer to a cutting board. Dip a very sharp kitchen knife in hot water and wipe it clean. Cut the rolls in thick slices. Discard the banana leaves.

6. **Sandwich assembly:** Use 1 baguette per serving. Cut lengthwise into the baguette and remove some of the crumb. Spread a thin layer of softened butter on one side and drizzle Maggi Seasoning on the other. Add the sliced *chả lụa*. Drizzle the inside of the baguette with Vegetarian Dipping Sauce (*Nước Chấm Chay*; see Chapter 6) and Sriracha hot sauce, to taste. Fill the sandwich with thin slices of jalapeño and the condiment(s) of your choice, such as Pickled Vietnamese Cabbage (*Dưa Muối*) and Pickled Carrots and Daikon (*Đồ Chua*) (see Chapter 6 for both condiments). Close the sandwich tightly.

WRAPPER ALTERNATIVES   You can find frozen banana leaves in most Asian markets. If not, you could use aluminum foil, undyed 100 percent cotton small fabric sheets, or plastic wrap in their place.

GREEN JACKFRUIT

Mít Kho Tương

YIELDS 6 SERVINGS

Green jackfruit is used in Vietnamese cuisine as a substitute for meat because of its fibrous texture, similar to shredded pork. In this recipe it's flavored with dark soy sauce and mixed with fried tofu for added protein.

8 ounces firm tofu

¼ cup canola oil

1 (1-pound) frozen unripe green jackfruit, thawed

½ teaspoon red chile powder

2 tablespoons hoisin sauce

2 cloves garlic, finely minced

1 tablespoon fresh ginger, julienned, cut about 1" long

1 (3") leek (white part only), chopped

1 cup shiitake mushrooms, sliced

1 teaspoon chile garlic sauce

1½ tablespoons Chinese brown sugar (*đường thẻ*) (or regular brown sugar)

3 tablespoons dark soy sauce

1 (12-ounce) can coconut soda (*nước dừa*), or fresh coconut water (or plain water)

½ teaspoon mushroom seasoning salt (*bột nêm*) (or regular salt)

½ teaspoon black pepper, freshly ground

4 sprigs cilantro, chopped

1. **Preparing the tofu:** Dice the tofu into 1½" cubes. In a wok, heat 2 tablespoons of the canola oil. Pan-fry the pieces of tofu until golden on all sides. The tofu should have a nice fried outer crust and still be moist inside. Transfer the tofu onto paper towels, leaving as much oil as possible in the wok. Set aside.

2. **Preparing the jackfruit:** Remove the outer rind and cut the fruit into large pieces. Soak in cold salted water for 30 minutes, then drain. Cut into 2" pieces (the pieces will shrink a bit once they're cooked). Blanch in boiling water for 1 minute and drain. Pat dry using paper towels. In the same wok, heat the oil that was left in the pan. Once the oil is hot, fry the pieces of jackfruit for 3–4 minutes until lightly golden. Transfer to a mixing bowl, leaving as much oil as possible in the wok. Add red chile powder and hoisin sauce to the bowl. Toss the fruit until it is well coated with these ingredients.

3. **Braising the tofu and jackfruit:** In the same wok, add more oil if necessary. Add the garlic and ginger. As the garlic becomes slightly golden, add the leek and cook for 2 minutes until softened. Add the tofu and shiitake mushrooms. Add the chile garlic sauce, *đường thẻ* (or brown sugar), and soy sauce. Stir-fry for 1 minute, then add the jackfruit. Immediately add coconut soda or coconut water. Bring to a boil, then lower the heat to a simmer. Stir frequently until all the liquid is absorbed. Season with mushroom seasoning salt. Finish with black pepper and cilantro.

4. **Sandwich assembly:** Use 1 baguette per serving. Cut lengthwise into the baguette and remove some of the crumb. Spread a thin layer of softened butter on one side. Add pieces of jackfruit and tofu to the sandwich. Drizzle the inside of the baguette with Vegetarian Dipping Sauce (*Nước Chấm Chay*; see Chapter 6). Add the condiment(s) of your choice, such as thinly sliced cucumbers and jalapeño peppers, and Pickled Carrots and Daikon (*Đồ Chua*; see Chapter 6). Garnish with 2 sprigs of cilantro. Close the sandwich tightly.

GREEN JACKFRUIT   Make sure to look for green jackfruit, which can be found in any Asian specialty markets or online. It can be frozen, in brine, or in water. Ripe yellow jackfruit won't work for this recipe, as it tastes sweet and has a gooey, sticky texture, far from a meat-like texture. If you're lucky to have fresh green jackfruit available, consider using disposable food service gloves and an inexpensive knife kept exclusively for cutting fruits such as jackfruit or durian. Once the fruit is cut, sap is released and there's a sticky substance that is very difficult to remove. (Note: Seeds from green jackfruit are edible because they're soft.)

LEMONGRASS TOFU

Tàu Hũ Xào Xả

YIELDS 4 SERVINGS

Lemongrass is a wonderfully fragrant herb. If prepared and cooked properly, it adds not only flavor but also great texture to any dish. Even though tofu is pretty bland by itself, lemongrass, along with shredded daikon, provides a unique, irresistible flavor.

1 (12-ounce) package firm tofu

3 tablespoons vegetable oil (or any neutral oil)

1½ fresh lemongrass stalks

1½ tablespoons palm sugar (or light brown sugar), freshly grated

½ teaspoon red chile powder

2 cloves garlic, finely minced

2 teaspoons mushroom seasoning salt (*bột nêm*) (or regular salt)

1 green Thai chile, stemmed, seeded, and finely chopped

1 small daikon, shredded (use the thickest grater)

2 teaspoons black bean sauce

2 tablespoons vegetarian mushroom-flavored stir-fry sauce

1 tablespoon soy sauce, to taste

¾ teaspoon black pepper, freshly ground

2 tablespoons Thai basil leaves, plus more for garnish

1. **Preparing the tofu:** Cut the tofu into 1" slices. In a wok, heat 2 tablespoons of the vegetable oil. Pan-fry the pieces of tofu on both sides until golden. The tofu should have a nice fried outer crust and still be moist inside. Transfer the tofu onto paper towels. Once the tofu pieces are cool enough to handle, cut them into thin threads. Set aside.

2. **Preparing the lemongrass:** Wash the lemongrass. Remove the white powder from the leaves. Cut the stalks in half. Crush the younger part (the part close to the root) with the back of a chef's knife and set it aside (you can use it for making broth). Cut the remainder of the stalks into extremely thin slices. In a mortar and pestle, grind the thin slices of lemongrass, then transfer to a mini food processor. Process into a fine moist powder. Spoon out 3 tablespoons and store the rest (see sidebar).

3. **Making lemongrass spice blend:** In a mortar and pestle, grind the lemongrass, sugar, red chile powder, 1 clove of the garlic, 1 teaspoon of the mushroom seasoning salt, and chopped Thai chile into a smooth paste.

4. **Making lemongrass tofu:** Add the remaining oil to the wok. Once the oil is hot, add the remaining clove of garlic. Cook until slightly golden, then add the shredded tofu and ⅔ of the lemongrass mixture. Stir-fry until the lemongrass coats the tofu evenly. Transfer the tofu to a platter, leaving as much oil as possible in the wok. Add the daikon to the wok. Add black bean sauce, mushroom stir-fry sauce, soy sauce, and black pepper. Stir-fry until softened. Return the tofu to the wok and add the reserved lemongrass mixture. Stir constantly and cook for 2–3 minutes. Check seasoning. Add more mushroom seasoning salt if necessary. Sprinkle with 2 tablespoons Thai basil. Toss well.

5. **Sandwich assembly:** Use 1 baguette per serving. Cut lengthwise into the baguette, removing some of the soft crumb. Spread a thin layer of softened butter on both sides. Fill the sandwich with lemongrass tofu, Beet Pickles (*Củ Cải Đường Muối Chua*; see Chapter 6), thinly sliced cucumbers, and shredded iceberg lettuce. Garnish with cilantro and Thai basil leaves. Close the sandwich tightly.

STORING LEMONGRASS Lemongrass can be found in most ethnic markets. It's sold in bulk in bunches of several stalks, so plan to make other dishes using lemongrass. You can store it loosely wrapped in paper towels in the refrigerator. Or, store finely chopped lemongrass in the freezer by placing a few tablespoons in an ice cube tray for future use.

SEAWEED TOFU

Cá Chiên Chay

YIELDS 8 SERVINGS

Cá Chiên Chay ("vegetarian fried fish" in Vietnamese) is a vegan alternative to the traditional steamed fish. The mock fish consists of tofu skin (*tàu hũ ky*), firm tofu, and seaweed. The result is surprisingly delicious. You might want to give this dish, typical of the Buddhist diet, a try; it is healthy, yet very tasty.

16 ounces frozen rolled tofu skin, plus 4 reserved sheets, thawed

1½ (16-ounce) packages firm tofu

1 teaspoon salt

3 tablespoons vegetable oil

2 teaspoons freshly grated ginger

1 teaspoon mushroom seasoning salt (*bột nêm*) (or regular salt)

1 teaspoon sugar

1 tablespoon soy sauce

4 toasted nori sheets, as needed

1 teaspoon white pepper, freshly ground

1 cup Vegetarian Dipping Sauce (*Nước Chấm Chay*; see Chapter 6)

1. **Preparing the firm tofu:** Soak the 4 reserved sheets of tofu skin in water. Pat dry. On a flat surface lined with a kitchen towel, place the tofu skin so it overlaps, forming a large rectangle, and set aside. Cut the firm tofu into 1" slices. Blanch the tofu slices for about 3–4 minutes in boiling salted water. Drain the liquid. Let the tofu cool a little. Once the tofu is cool enough and has dried thoroughly, arrange the firm tofu slices into a large rectangle on the sheets of tofu skin.

2. **Preparing the tofu skin:** Fill a large pot three-quarters full with water. Bring to a boil. Add 1 teaspoon salt and enough cold water so the water becomes lukewarm. Add the remaining tofu skin left from the 16-ounce package and soak for 4–5 minutes. Drain and let cool for 15 minutes. Pat dry with a towel, removing as much moisture as possible. In a large pan, heat the oil. Once the oil is hot, add ginger and cook until fragrant. Add the freshly soaked tofu skin, mushroom seasoning salt, sugar, and soy sauce. Stir-fry for 10 minutes until the liquid evaporates completely. Mix well. Let cool for 1 hour before wrapping.

3. **Assembly time:** Place the nori sheets on the rectangle of firm tofu. Wet your hands with warm water and spread handfuls of the tofu skin mixture on the nori (covering about ¾ of the nori surface). Spread it evenly, stopping 2½" inside the edges of the rectangle. Gently press so the mixture adheres to the nori sheets. Using the towel underneath as a guide, tightly and slowly roll the towel away from you, as you would for a jelly roll (the roll is made with the firm tofu as the outside). Press gently with both hands for about 10 seconds to seal the end of the roll. Wrap the roll in the sheets of tofu skin (wrap the tofu skin sheet that was underneath around the firm tofu). Tie the roll with twine or string.

4. **Steaming the tofu roll:** Pour water in the bottom of a steamer to a depth of at least 3". Place the rack in the steamer. Bring the water to a boil, then lower the heat to medium-high. Place the roll in the steamer; cover and steam for about 30–40 minutes. The roll should be soft and tender but still firm. Remove from the steamer. Let cool a little. Chill in the refrigerator for at least 2 hours. Remove and discard the tofu skin wrapping. Transfer to a cutting board. Dip a very sharp kitchen knife in hot water and wipe it clean. Cut the rolls in thick slices. Season with Vegetarian Dipping Sauce (*Nước Chấm Chay*; see Chapter 6).

5. **Sandwich assembly:** Use 1 baguette per serving. Cut lengthwise into the baguette and remove some of the crumb. Spread a thin layer of softened butter on one side and drizzle Maggi Seasoning or Vegetarian Dipping Sauce (*Nước Chấm Chay*; see Chapter 6) on the other. Add the sliced *cá chiên chay*. Fill the sandwich with thin slices of jalapeño, shredded iceberg lettuce, and the condiment(s) of your choice, such as Pickled Bean Sprouts (*Dưa Giá Với Hẹ Trái Táo Xanh*) and Pickled Papaya (*Gỏi Đu Đủ*) (see Chapter 6 for both condiments). Garnish with 2 sprigs of cilantro. Close the sandwich tightly.

WHEAT GLUTEN STIR-FRY

Mì Căn Xào Nấm Bào Ngư

YIELDS 6 SERVINGS

Vegetarian mock duck meat is made of wheat gluten dough that is deep-fried then sautéed in black bean chile garlic sauce. A few seasonal vegetables such as abalone mushrooms (*nấm bào ngư*), bamboo shoots (*măng*), carrots (*cà rốt*), and string beans (*đậu ve*) are mixed in to add color to the vegan dish. The chewy texture is so similar to real meat you won't miss having animal protein.

1 yellow onion

1 cup green beans

1 large carrot

1 abalone mushroom (King oyster mushroom)

2 tablespoons peanut oil (or any neutral oil)

2 cloves fresh garlic, crushed and finely minced

½ teaspoon mushroom seasoning salt (*bột nêm*) (or regular salt)

½ cup water

1 (10-ounce) can fried gluten, rinsed and drained

½ cup marinated bamboo shoots, sliced

1 cup combined red and green bell peppers, diced

1 cup abalone mushrooms, diced

1 teaspoon black bean garlic sauce

1¼ teaspoons chile garlic sauce, to taste

1 teaspoon grated palm sugar (or granulated sugar)

2 tablespoons soy sauce

¼ teaspoon black pepper, freshly ground

¼ cup Thai basil leaves, torn in half

1 tablespoon cilantro, chopped

1. **Preparing the onion:** Cut the onion in half. Finely chop one half and cut the other into thin wedges.

2. **Preparing the vegetables:** Wash and pat dry the green beans. Trim the ends. Cut them into 1½"-long pieces. Trim the carrot and peel them. Cut them into quarters lengthwise, then cut into 1½"-long pieces. Repeat the same procedure for the mushroom. All vegetables should be the same size.

3. **Cooking the beans:** Heat the oil in a wok. Add the garlic and cook until slightly golden. Add the green beans. Toss well, leaving the heat at the highest setting for about 3 minutes, until the color changes and they become shiny. Add mushroom seasoning salt (this step will ensure a bright green color for the beans). Transfer to a platter.

4. **Assembly time:** Add more oil to the wok if necessary. Add the chopped onions and carrots. Cook until the onions are caramelized. Add water, cover, and cook for 4 minutes until carrots are softened. Add the gluten, bamboo shoots, red and green bell peppers, abalone mushrooms, black bean garlic sauce, chile garlic sauce, sugar, and soy sauce. Sauté until well combined. Add the onion wedges and the string beans. Stir-fry for about 2 minutes. Check the doneness of the carrots (add a little water if not fully cooked) and cook until softened. Sprinkle with black pepper. Finish with Thai basil leaves and cilantro. Mix well and cover until ready to serve. Keep on the stove for about 5 minutes.

5. **Sandwich assembly:** Use 1 baguette per serving. Cut lengthwise into the baguette and remove some of the crumb. Spread a thin layer of softened butter on one side. Add the wheat gluten and vegetables. Drizzle the inside of the baguette with Vegetarian Dipping Sauce (*Nước Chấm Chay*; see Chapter 6) and Sriracha hot sauce (to taste). Fill the sandwich with thinly sliced jalapeño and the condiment(s) of your choice, such as Pickled Vietnamese Cabbage (*Dưa Muối*) and Pickled Carrots and Daikon (*Đồ Chua*) (see Chapter 6 for both condiments). Garnish with 2 sprigs of cilantro. Close the sandwich tightly.

VEGETARIAN *CHAR SIU*

Xá Xíu Chay

YIELDS 6 SERVINGS

This vegetarian version of *char siu* is not only as flavorful and colorful as the one with meat, but it also sheds the fatty elements real meat can bring. Shiitake mushrooms help add a thick, meaty texture to the dish.

1 (2") piece fresh ginger

2 (12-ounce) packages firm tofu

3 tablespoons canola oil

¼ cup date syrup (or honey)

¼ cup soy sauce

⅓ cup hoisin sauce (or oyster sauce)

1 teaspoon five-spice powder

1 pinch red food coloring (optional)

2 tablespoons dry sherry (optional)

1 red onion, ½ chopped, ½ cut into thin wedges

2 cloves garlic, cut in thirds

1½ cups shiitake mushrooms, coarsely chopped

½ cup water

2 teaspoons chile garlic sauce, to taste

1 teaspoon sesame oil

½ teaspoon salt, or to taste

¼ teaspoon black pepper, freshly ground

1 tablespoon cilantro, finely chopped

1 teaspoon sesame oil

1. **Preparing the ginger:** Peel the ginger with a paring knife, thinly slice it, then cut into long matchsticks. Set aside.

2. **Preparing the tofu:** Cut the tofu into 1" slices. In a wok, heat 2 tablespoons of the canola oil. Pan-fry the pieces of tofu on both sides until golden. The tofu should have a nice fried outer crust and still be moist inside. Transfer the tofu to paper towels. Once the tofu pieces are cool enough to handle, cut them into quarters. Set aside.

3. **Making *char siu* sauce:** In a small saucepan, combine the date syrup (or honey) and soy sauce. Bring to a boil, then reduce heat and simmer for 2–3 minutes. Turn off the heat. Add hoisin sauce (or oyster sauce), five-spice powder, red food coloring (if using), and dry sherry (if using). Stir well and set aside.

4. **Assembly time:** Add the rest of the oil to the wok. Once it's hot, add the chopped red onion. Cook until fragrant, then add the garlic and ginger. As the garlic becomes slightly golden, add the tofu and stir-fry until fragrant. Transfer the tofu and onion mixture to a platter, leaving as much oil as possible in the wok. Add the mushrooms. Sauté for 3–4 minutes until shiny. Transfer to a platter. Add the *char siu* sauce and water. Once the sauce thickens, add the fried tofu and chile garlic sauce. Stir-fry for about 3–4 minutes. Return the shiitake mushrooms and add the onion wedges to the wok. Stir constantly. Check seasoning. Add salt and pepper. Sprinkle with cilantro. Toss well. Drizzle with sesame oil.

5. **Sandwich assembly:** Use 1 baguette per serving. Cut lengthwise into the baguette and remove some of the crumb. Spread a thin layer of softened butter on one side. Add the *char siu* tofu, thin onion, and mushroom mixture. Drizzle the inside of the baguette with Vegetarian Dipping Sauce (*Nước Chấm Chay*; see Chapter 6) and Sriracha hot sauce (to taste). Fill the sandwich with thin slices of jalapeño and the condiment(s) of your choice, such as Beet Pickles (*Củ Cải Đường Muối Chua*; see Chapter 6). Garnish with 2 sprigs of cilantro. Close the sandwich tightly.

HOMEMADE FIVE-SPICE POWDER   To create your own five-spice powder, combine ½ stick of Saigonese cinnamon, 1 star anise, 2 cloves, ½ teaspoon fennel seed, and ¼ teaspoon of Sichuan pepper in a small bowl. Dry roast the contents of the bowl in a hot pan over the stove. Stir the spices using chopsticks until they become fragrant (for 3 minutes over high heat). Let cool. Grind the spices into a fine powder using a food processor or spice grinder.

SPICY EGGPLANT TOFU

Cà Tím Xào Tàu Hũ

YIELDS 6 SERVINGS

If you're looking for a vegetarian stir fry, Japanese eggplant and tofu might be your quick fix. The sauce consists of basic Asian ingredients such as soy sauce, chile black bean sauce, palm sugar, and fresh ginger. The ginger and black bean sauce enhance the bland eggplant and tofu. Pair this with crunchy pickles and enjoy a dazzling tofu *bánh mì*.

1 (12-ounce) package firm tofu

3 tablespoons vegetable oil (or any neutral oil), as needed

1 (2") piece fresh ginger

3 Japanese eggplants

1 teaspoon salt

1 tablespoon chile black bean sauce

¼ cup soy sauce

1 teaspoon palm sugar, freshly grated (or light brown sugar)

2 shallots, sliced

1 teaspoon toasted sesame oil, optional

½ teaspoon mushroom seasoning salt (*bột nêm*) (or regular salt), or to taste

⅓ teaspoon black pepper, freshly ground

1 tablespoon sesame seeds, lightly toasted

1. **Preparing the tofu:** Cut the tofu into 1½" slices, then into 1½" sticks. In a wok, heat 2 tablespoons of the vegetable oil. Pan-fry the pieces of tofu until golden on all sides. The tofu should have a nice fried outer crust and still be moist inside. Transfer the tofu onto paper towels, leaving as much oil as possible in the wok. Set aside.

2. **Preparing the ginger:** Clean the chunk of ginger, carefully removing any dirt. Peel the ginger root with a paring knife or the edge of a spoon, then chop very finely.

3. **Preparing the eggplants:** Trim the eggplants. Cut them in half lengthwise and slice them into 5–6 pieces. Place a cooling rack on top of a cookie sheet (to collect the excess moisture). Place the eggplant pieces on the rack and sprinkle with salt. Let sit for about 20 minutes, then pat dry using paper towels. Drizzle the eggplants with a little oil and sprinkle with about 1½ tablespoons ginger. Toss well.

4. **For the stir-fry sauce:** In a small bowl, combine the black bean sauce, soy sauce, and sugar. Stir well.

5. **Assembly time:** Add more oil to the wok if necessary. Add the rest of the ginger and the shallots. Cook until fragrant, then add the eggplant pieces. Ensure that the eggplant pieces are lightly coated in oil (no need to use a lot). Once a dry outer crust is formed, drizzle with the soy sauce mixture. Add the tofu pieces. Toss well, cover with a lid, lower the heat to low, and cook for 5–8 minutes until soft and tender. Once all the liquid at the bottom of the wok evaporates, check that the eggplant is tender; if not fully cooked, add more water and continue cooking. Drizzle with toasted sesame oil (if used). Check seasoning; add mushroom seasoning salt and black pepper. Turn off the heat, but keep the wok on the stove for about 5 minutes. Sprinkle with sesame seeds.

6. **Sandwich assembly:** Use 1 baguette per serving. Cut lengthwise into the baguette and remove some of the crumb. Spread a thin layer of softened butter on one side. Add pieces of eggplant and tofu to the sandwich. Drizzle the inside of the baguette with Vegetarian Dipping Sauce (*Nước Chấm Chay*; see Chapter 6). Add sliced cucumbers, thinly sliced jalapeño pepper, and the condiment(s) of your choice, such as Pickled Carrots and Daikon (*Đồ Chua*; see Chapter 6). Garnish with 2 sprigs of cilantro. Close the sandwich tightly.

AVOCADO, GINGER, AND GRAPEFRUIT SANDWICH

Bánh Mì Bưởi Bơ

YIELDS 3 SERVINGS

As with many simple dishes, attention to detail is the difference between drab and delicious. This healthy *bánh mì* consists of mixed fried tofu (*tàu hủ chiên*), avocado (*trái bơ*), ginger (*gừng*), Ruby Red grapefruit (*bưởi ruột đỏ*), Vietnamese cilantro (*ngò rí*), lettuce (*xà lách*), tomato (*cà chua*), Cheddar cheese (*pho mát*), and mayonnaise (*sôt ma do ne*).

1 avocado, peeled, pitted, and sliced

Juice of 1 lime, freshly squeezed

2 Ruby Red grapefruits

¾ teaspoon salt

½ teaspoon white pepper

1 (12-ounce) package firm tofu

2 tablespoons peanut oil (or any neutral oil), as needed

2 shallots, sliced

2 teaspoons freshly grated ginger

1 tablespoon candied ginger, finely chopped

2 cloves Pickled Garlic (*Tỏi Chua Ngọt*; see Chapter 6), thinly sliced

2 tablespoons Vietnamese cilantro (*ngò rí*), chopped

1½ cups iceberg lettuce, shredded

2 tomatoes, seeded and cut into thin wedges

¼ cup Vegetarian Dipping Sauce (*Nước Chấm Chay*; see Chapter 6)

1 tablespoon sesame oil

10 slices Cheddar cheese

1. **Preparing the avocado:** Slice the avocado in half and remove the pit. Using a mandoline or a sharp chef's knife, slice the avocado into thick ribbons for a pretty presentation. Transfer to a plate, removing the peel for each slice. Cut the slices in half lengthwise. Drizzle with lime juice to avoid oxidation.

2. **Segmenting the grapefruit:** Peel each grapefruit and divide in half. Remove the membrane wall on one side around a segment. Apply a little pressure on the segment with your thumb to separate the segment along the next membrane (you could also use a paring knife, but don't cut the fruit; use the knife as a separator). Free the segment and gently pull it away from the fruit so it remains intact, removing all the membrane. Repeat and remove the rest of the segments. This technique releases the flesh and spills less juice. Transfer the grapefruit segments with as much juice as possible into a mixing bowl. Season with salt and white pepper.

3. **Preparing the tofu:** Cut the tofu into 1½" slices, then into 1½" sticks. Heat the oil in a wok. Pan-fry tofu until golden on all sides. The tofu should have a nice fried outer crust and still be moist inside. Transfer the tofu to paper towels, leaving as much oil as possible in the wok.

4. **Frying the shallots:** Peel and slice the shallots. Reheat the oil in the wok (add more if necessary). Working in batches (for extra crispness), add the shallots and fry for 5 minutes until crisp and golden brown. Transfer to a platter lined with paper towels. Add more oil between batches if necessary.

5. **Assembly time:** In the same bowl with the grapefruit segments, combine the tofu, shallots, grated ginger, candied ginger, pickled garlic, cilantro, lettuce, and tomatoes. Add 2 tablespoons *nước chấm chay* and the sesame oil. Gently toss until all the ingredients are coated with the dressing.

6. **Sandwich assembly:** Use 1 baguette per serving. Cut lengthwise into the baguette and remove some of the crumb. Spread a thin layer of Lime Mayonnaise (*Sốt Ma Dô Ne*; see Chapter 6) on one side and arrange slices of Cheddar cheese on the other. Add the grapefruit mixture to the sandwich. Top with thinly sliced avocado. Add thinly sliced jalapeño pepper and the condiment(s) of your choice, such as Pickled Vietnamese Cabbage (*Dưa Muối*; see Chapter 6). Close the sandwich tightly.

CHAPTER 3

POULTRY SANDWICHES

Whether they're boiled (*gỏi gà*), sautéed in lemongrass (*gà xào xả*), or stewed in a spicy turmeric gravy (*ca ri gà*), Vietnamese poultry dishes are not short on flavor. You can use regular chickens from your local market, but if you live near an Asian specialty store, try using special Vietnamese chickens, called *gà đi bộ* (it literally translates to "walking chickens"). They're free-range chickens, and the texture of the meat is firmer than regular chicken.

The beauty of the poultry recipes in this chapter is that you will get two meals for the price of one. Serve the meat portion for dinner, and then use the leftovers the next day in delicious *bánh mì* sandwiches. Chicken night will never be the same!

These recipes are for typical poultry *bánh mì* fillings, ones you would find in a *bánh mì* shop. In general, use 1 small authentic Vietnamese baguette per serving, or ⅓ of a larger French baguette. (Try making your own! See the Vietnamese Baguette: *Bánh Mì Baguette* recipe in Chapter 1.) For each recipe, the final step includes sandwich assembly instructions. You can choose to use the suggested ingredients, or mix and match your favorite flavors to taste. The listed ingredients are a general guide, and you can customize your sandwiches for a unique *bánh mì* experience every time.

CHICKEN SALAD

Gỏi Gà

YIELDS 4 SERVINGS

The secret to a no-fail Vietnamese chicken salad is in flavoring the broth before boiling the chicken. This is the one chance you have to infuse additional flavor into the meat. For texture, shredded white cabbage is added, along with Vietnamese herbs.

1 red onion (or shallot for a stronger flavor)

2 teaspoons brown sugar

4 limes

1 (2") chunk fresh ginger

2 tablespoons water, plus 7 quarts

3 fried yellow onions, not too browned

¼ teaspoon red chile powder

1 whole chicken

4 chicken thighs and drumsticks

½ daikon, peeled

1 whole yellow onion, peeled

1 (1") chunk rock sugar

2 teaspoons mushroom seasoning salt (*bột nêm*) (or regular salt)

1½ teaspoons salt, divided use

¼ teaspoon black pepper, freshly ground

¼ cup peanuts (optional)

1½ tablespoons sugar

3 cloves Pickled Garlic (*Tỏi Chua Ngọt*; see Chapter 6), finely minced

1 tablespoon soy sauce

1 red Thai bird chile (optional), stemmed, seeded, and thinly sliced

1 tablespoon dried fried shallot (store-bought)

2 cups Chinese cabbage, shredded

3 sprigs *ngò gai*, chopped

3 tablespoons Thai basil, chopped

3 tablespoons Vietnamese mint, chopped

3 sprigs *rau răm* (Vietnamese coriander), chopped

1. **Pickling the red onion:** Peel and thinly slice the red onion; mince finely. Place the sliced onion in a bowl, sprinkle with brown sugar, and drizzle with the juice of half of a lime. Toss well. Set aside.

2. **Making ginger paste:** Clean the ginger. Peel the ginger root with a paring knife and finely chop it. Place the chopped ginger in a mini-blender, adding about 2 tablespoons (or more) of water to make a smooth paste. Spoon out about 2 teaspoons. Set aside.

3. **Preparing the chicken:** Bring about 7 quarts of water to a boil. Add the fried onions and red chile powder. Boil for about 5 minutes. Add the whole chicken, thighs, and drumsticks to the onion broth. Cook for about 10–12 minutes. Remove the whole chicken from the pot. Let it cool a bit until you can handle it without discomfort. Make several deep diagonal incisions throughout the bird's flesh. Place the chicken back in the broth. Add the daikon, the whole onion, rock sugar, and mushroom seasoning salt. Bring to a boil and let the chicken simmer for another 30 minutes until the whole onion and daikon are soft and tender. Season with 1 teaspoon salt. Bring back to a boil, then immediately lower the heat to a gentle boil. Cook for another 10–12 minutes. Remove the whole chicken and chicken pieces. Let them cool a bit until you can handle them without discomfort. Shred the meat. Sprinkle with black pepper. Set the meat aside on a platter. Reserve the chicken broth for another recipe.

4. **Peanuts:** In a mortar and pestle, coarsely crush the peanuts.

5. *Gỏi* **sauce (salad dressing):** In a bowl, combine juice of remaining limes, sugar, ½ teaspoon salt, pickled garlic, ginger paste, and soy sauce. Mix well.

6. **Finalizing the salad:** In a large bowl, combine the shredded chicken, red Thai chile, and dried fried shallot. Add the shredded cabbage, *ngò gai*, and pickled red onion with its liquid. When you're ready to serve, drizzle the chicken mixture with *gỏi* sauce (salad dressing). Add all the chopped herbs. Toss well. Season with more salt (if needed) and the remaining black pepper. Sprinkle with the peanuts (if using).

CHICKEN SALAD: *Gỏi Gà*

LEMONGRASS CHICKEN

Gà Nướng Xào Xả

YIELDS 8 SERVINGS

Lemongrass chicken is a delicious and easy-to-prepare Vietnamese meat dish. The chicken pieces are marinated overnight to guarantee optimum tenderness, and then they're mixed with finely chopped lemongrass. The mix of spices provides a lovely fragrance and boosts the taste of lemongrass, which has hints of sweet lemon and a touch of ginger. Lemongrass really adds a distinctive flavor, but if it isn't ground properly into a fine, moist powder, this dish can easily be ruined. For a vegetarian equivalent of this recipe, check out Lemongrass Tofu (*Tàu Hũ Xào Xả*) in Chapter 2.

2 pounds chicken breasts, boneless and skinless

1½ teaspoons red chile powder

½ teaspoon baking powder

2 teaspoons freshly grated green papaya with its seeds

Juice of 1 lemon

5 tablespoons vegetable oil

2 stalks lemongrass

1½ tablespoons granulated sugar

1 tablespoon mushroom seasoning salt (*bột nêm*) (or regular salt)

1 yellow onion, cut into small wedges

2 shallots, finely chopped

2 cloves garlic, finely minced

¾ teaspoon turmeric powder

2 jalapeños, sliced

2 tablespoons coconut milk (optional)

⅓ cup chicken stock, as needed

1 tablespoon Fish Sauce (*Nước Mắm Chấm*; see Chapter 6) (optional)

1 teaspoon salt

¾ teaspoon black pepper, freshly ground

2 tablespoons Thai basil, for garnish

1. **Marinating the chicken:** The night before serving, trim the fat around the bottom of the breasts if there is any. Wash the chicken breasts and pat them dry with paper towels. Cut chicken into 1½"–2" cubes. Gather the pieces in a mixing bowl. Season the chicken with ¾ teaspoon of the red chile powder. Add the baking powder and grated papaya. Mix well. Place the chicken in a large bowl or a sealable zip-top bag. Drizzle with 1 tablespoon of lemon juice and about 2 tablespoons of the oil. Marinate in the refrigerator overnight.

2. **Preparing the lemongrass:** Wash the lemongrass, removing the white powder from the leaves. Cut the stalks in half. Crush the younger part (the part closest to the root) with the back of a chef's knife and set it aside (you can use it for making broth). Cut the remainder of the stalks into extremely thin slices. In a mortar and pestle, grind the thin slices of lemongrass, then transfer to a mini food processor. Process into a fine moist powder. Spoon out 3 tablespoons and store the extra lemongrass (see sidebar in Lemongrass Tofu recipe, Chapter 2).

3. **Making lemongrass spice blend:** In a small bowl, combine 3 tablespoons ground lemongrass, sugar, 2 teaspoons of the mushroom seasoning salt, and the remaining chile powder.

4. **Cooking the vegetables:** Pat the meat dry one more time, again using paper towels. In a large nonstick pan, heat about 2–3 tablespoons of oil. Add the onion wedges and cook on high heat for about 2–3 minutes until slightly golden. The onions should still be crunchy. Transfer the onions to a plate and set aside. In the same pan, cook the shallots on high heat until slightly golden. Lower the heat to medium-low and cook until soft and tender, about 6 minutes. Transfer to another bowl. Add the rest of the oil (1 tablespoon) to the pan. Once the oil is hot, add the minced garlic and cook until slightly golden. Increase the heat to the highest setting, add ⅔ of the quantity of the lemongrass spice blend, and cook until slightly golden.

5. **Cooking the chicken:** Pan-sear each side of the pieces of chicken in the same pan for about 1½ minutes (a total of about 9 minutes) until golden. Season with turmeric powder and remaining mushroom seasoning salt. Stir constantly and cook for about 5 minutes until the color changes. The

lemongrass blend should coat the pieces of chicken. Once the chicken is golden on each side, add the remaining lemongrass mixture, shallots, and jalapeños. Stir well. Add the coconut milk (if using, for a richer mouth-feel) and chicken stock. Once the liquid evaporates, add *nước mắm* (if using). Adjust seasoning. Add salt and black pepper. Cook for another 15 minutes. Finish with remaining lemon juice, Thai basil, and reserved onions. Stir well.

6. **Sandwich assembly:** Use 1 baguette per serving. Cut lengthwise into the baguette and remove some of the crumb. Spread a thin layer of softened butter on one side and Lime Mayonnaise (*Sốt Ma Dô Ne*; see Chapter 6) on the other. Add the chicken. Fill the sandwich with thin slices of jalapeño, cucumber slices, and the condiment(s) of your choice, such as Pickled Mango (*Gỏi Xoài Xanh*; see Chapter 6). Garnish with 2 sprigs of cilantro. Close the sandwich tightly.

LACQUERED DUCK

Vịt Tiềm

YIELDS 6 SERVINGS

The key to good Chinese roast duck is to create crispy skin while still keeping the meat moist and sweet. The duck is first brined for several days, then boiled and finally roasted and basted with a dark, sweet and salty marinade.

1 (3½-pound) whole duck, cleaned

1 tablespoon peppercorns, coarsely crushed

1½ tablespoons freshly grated ginger

4 teaspoons salt

2 tablespoons chile garlic sauce

2 tablespoons green papaya with its seeds, freshly ground

Juice of 1 lemon, squeezed; lemon halves reserved

2 drops red food coloring (optional)

¼ cup vegetable oil

1 large yellow onion, finely sliced

2 teaspoons five-spice powder

3 cloves garlic, freshly grated

1 tablespoon maltose (*đường mạch nha*) or sugar

⅓ cup honey

2 tablespoons rice vinegar

1 tablespoon soy sauce

3 green onions, halved crosswise

1 tablespoon butter, softened to room temperature

2 tablespoons dark molasses, plus extra for the infuser

1. **Separating the skin from the flesh:** First, make sure the skin of the duck is not punctured. Clean the duck thoroughly. Trim the fatty pieces near the bottom. Leave the skin on. Close the cavity at the bottom to get the skin to separate from the flesh. Insert an air pump hose into the neck hole from the chest side. (If you do not have one, try to delicately separate the flesh from the skin manually, without tearing the skin.) A bicycle air pump is the best way to inflate the duck and a clean way to separate the duck's skin from its flesh without tearing it. That way the brine is evenly distributed throughout the meat.

2. **Brining the poultry:** Combine the crushed peppercorns, 1 tablespoon ginger, 2 teapoons salt, chile garlic sauce, papaya, lemon juice, a few drops of red food coloring (if using), and the duck in a large bucket. Fill the bucket with ice water. Make sure the brine covers the duck (you might want to place a heavy weight on top to ensure the duck is submerged with the brine). Set aside in a cool area for at least 3 hours, preferably overnight. Stir frequently and add ice when necessary (there should always be ice in the water). Remove the duck from the liquid. Discard the brine.

3. **Caramelizing the onions:** In a medium-sized nonstick pan, heat 2 tablespoons oil and add the onion. Decrease the temperature to medium-low and cook for about 10–15 minutes. Drain the oil and reserve it for later use in this recipe.

4. **Boiling the duck:** Fill a large pot with water and bring to a boil. Add the caramelized onions and the duck. Cook for about 5 minutes. Drain and discard the water. Pat the duck dry with paper towels.

5. **Seasoning the bird:** In a bowl, combine the five-spice powder, 1 teaspoon salt, 1 tablespoon of the onion oil, ½ tablespoon ginger, garlic, maltose, and 1 tablespoon of the honey. Wearing disposable gloves, spread the mixture in the cavity and on the outside of the bird. Spread evenly. Place the duck on a vertical roasting stand (without the infuser) and cover the duck entirely with plastic wrap. Chill on the top shelf of the refrigerator for about 4 hours. Remove the duck. Discard the liquid at the bottom of the vertical stand. Wash the stand in hot soapy water.

6. **Roasting the duck:** Remove the duck 15 minutes before cooking to bring it back to room temperature. Pat dry one more time. Preheat the oven to 350°F. In a bowl, mix the remaining honey with rice vinegar and soy sauce. Brush the duck with the vinegar mixture using a silicone brush. Drizzle with a little reserved onion oil, then sprinkle about 1 teaspoon salt on the bird. Cover just the tip and shoulders with foil to prevent burning. Place on the rotisserie of your oven or in a roaster, or a vertical stand with an integrated infuser. (If using an infuser, place a little citrus juice, green onions, and molasses in the cup; stuff it with the remnant quarters of citrus; and then seal.) Place the duck on top and place the whole thing on a tray. Roast for 30 minutes. Lower the heat to 325°F and cook for another 10 minutes. Remove the foil. (If you do not have an infuser, use an empty tall soda can [23 fluid ounce size] or a roaster.)

7. **Basting:** In the microwave, melt 1 tablespoon butter with the molasses. Baste the bird with the butter mixture, using a silicone brush. Increase the temperature to 425°F for an additional 10 minutes to brown the duck. Remove from the oven and loosely cover the duck with aluminum foil so the skin remains crispy. Allow duck to rest for 15 minutes before carving. Separate the crispy skin, reserving it, and shred the meat.

8. **Sandwich assembly:** Use 1 baguette per serving. Cut lengthwise into the baguette and remove some of the crumb. Spread a thin layer of softened butter on one side and hoisin sauce on the other. Add the shredded duck meat with crispy skin. Fill the sandwich with thin slices of jalapeño, cucumber slices, shredded lettuce, and the condiment(s) of your choice, such as Pickled Bean Sprouts (*Dưa Giá Với Hẹ Trái Táo Xanh*; see Chapter 6). Garnish with 2 sprigs of cilantro. Close the sandwich tightly.

CARVING THE DUCK It's possible to use poultry shears to cut up all of the duck, but that's more difficult to do than it would be for a roasted chicken. (Be very careful if you do use them.) There is an easier way to carve a duck. Place some newspapers under a large wooden cutting board and place the duck on top of the board. Remove the wings and thighs with the poultry shears. Then use a cleaver to cut the bird in two lengthwise. Cut each half into 2" pieces and shred the meat with a knife, reserving the crispy skin.

LACQUERED DUCK: *Vịt Tiềm*

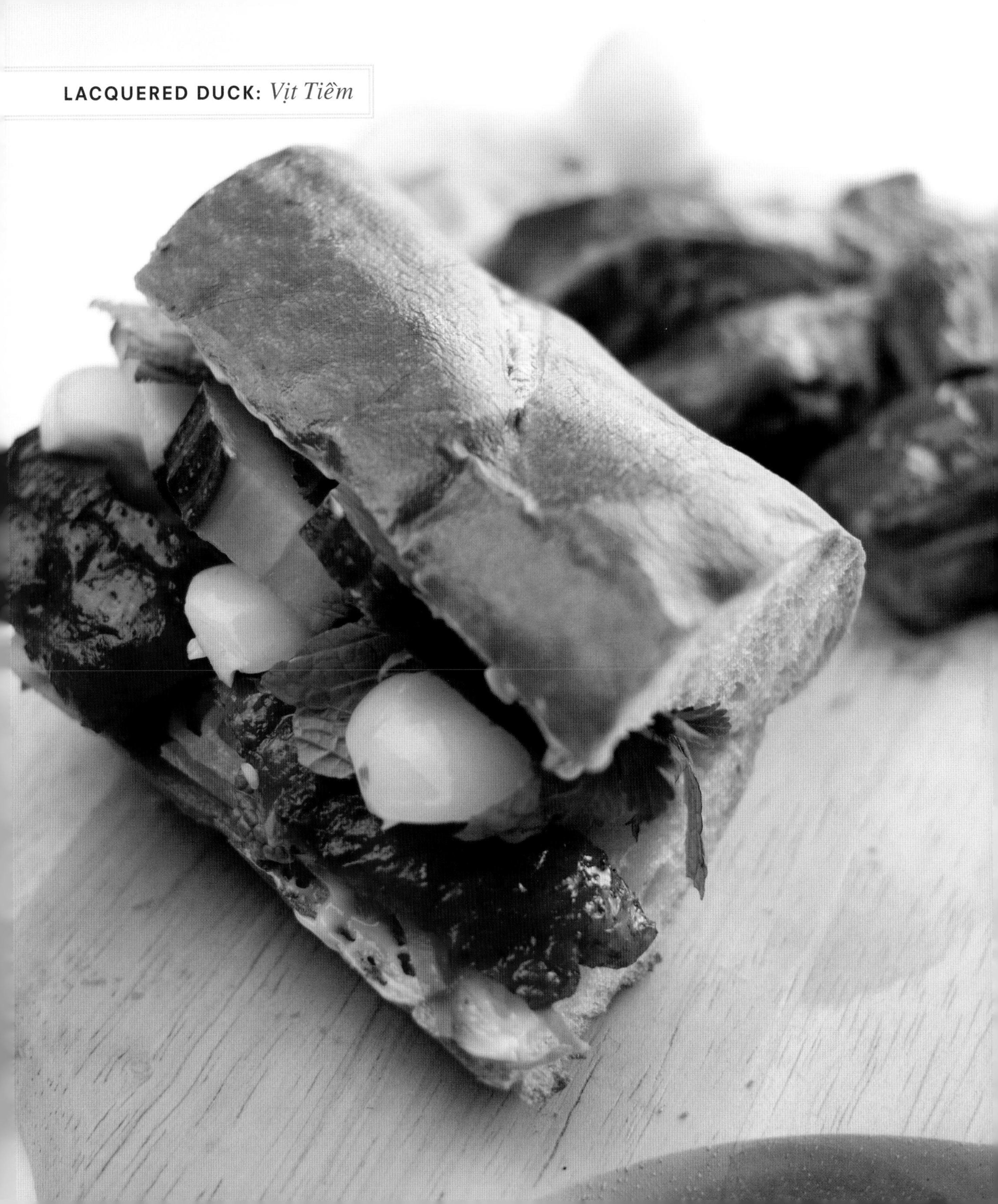

CHICKEN TERIYAKI

Gà Teriyaki

YIELDS 6 SERVINGS

This chicken preparation is reminiscent of Japanese chicken with teriyaki sauce. Flavorful dark meat from chicken thighs is grilled (or broiled), then brushed until shiny with a thick, sweet soy sauce marinade.

1 tablespoon grated green papaya (optional)

½ teaspoon cayenne powder

½ cup brown sugar

1 tablespoon salt

2 tablespoons rice wine (*rượu gạo nấu ăn*) (optional)

1 (2") piece ginger, freshly grated

1½ cups cold water

2 pounds boneless chicken thighs with skin on

¼ cup honey

3 cloves garlic, freshly grated

½ teaspoon wasabi paste

¼ cup coconut juice (or water)

2 tablespoons rice vinegar

Juice of 1 lime, freshly squeezed

⅔ cup soy sauce

3 tablespoons vegetable oil (or any neutral oil)

4 tablespoons chopped green onions, for garnish

2 tablespoons toasted sesame seeds

1 teaspoon sesame oil (optional)

1. **Marinating the chicken:** In a large mixing bowl, combine the grated papaya (if using), cayenne powder, 6 tablespoons brown sugar, 2 teaspoons salt, 1 tablespoon rice wine (if using), 1½ teaspoons grated ginger, and cold water. Stir well. Add the chicken pieces. Make sure the chicken is well coated. Cover with plastic wrap and refrigerate for at least 2 hours, preferably overnight.

2. **For the teriyaki sauce:** In a small saucepan, combine the honey, remaining grated ginger, garlic, wasabi paste, coconut juice (or water), rice vinegar, remaining 2 tablespoons brown sugar, lime juice, soy sauce, and 1 tablespoon rice wine (if using). Warm over low heat on the stove; the sugar should be completely dissolved. Reserve 2–3 tablespoons for basting the meat.

3. **Frying the chicken:** Preheat the oven to 450°F. Drain the chicken and thoroughly pat dry with paper towels. Brush an ovenproof, nonstick grill pan (preferably cast iron) with a generous layer of vegetable oil. Add the green onions. Cook until softened and fragrant but still green; transfer to a small bowl and set aside. Pat the chicken dry one more time. Using a brush, lightly coat the chicken pieces with vegetable oil. Once the oil in the pan is hot, place the chicken thighs in the pan (make sure the cast-iron pan is well-seasoned so the meat doesn't stick to the pan). Pan-sear for 2 minutes; flip and sear the other side, leaving the chicken in the pan. Wipe the pan as clean as possible with a paper towel, then add the teriyaki sauce. Cover the meat and reduce to the lowest setting. Cook for about 10 minutes, flipping the pieces of meat periodically until the liquid released during the cooking evaporates.

4. **Baking the chicken:** Quickly transfer the chicken to the oven and bake for 8 minutes (depending on the thickness of the meat). A thermometer should register 165°F in the thickest part of the chicken piece or the juice should run clear. Baste the chicken with the reserved teriyaki sauce; the chicken should be generously coated with sauce. Remove from the oven. Lightly cover with a sheet of aluminum foil. Let chicken rest for at least 15 minutes before serving. Cut into thick slices, ensuring all slices are basted in sauce. Sprinkle with sesame seeds. Drizzle with sesame oil (if using), and garnish with the reserved green onions.

5. **Sandwich assembly:** Use 1 baguette per serving. Cut lengthwise into the baguette and remove some of the crumb. Spread a thin layer of softened butter on one side and Lime Mayonnaise (*Sốt Ma Dô Ne*; see Chapter 6) on the other. Add the sliced teriyaki chicken. Fill the sandwich with thin slices of jalapeño and the condiment(s) of your choice, such as Pickled Vietnamese Cabbage (*Dưa Muối*) and Pickled Carrots and Daikon (*Đồ Chua*) (see Chapter 6 for both condiments). Garnish with 2 sprigs of cilantro. Close the sandwich tightly.

MAKING MEAT TENDERIZER   If you use the grated papaya for this recipe, you can make meat tenderizer from the rest of the fruit. Cube the remaining papaya and purée it along with its seeds in a blender, adding a little water to create a paste (about the consistency of apple sauce). Spoon about 2 teaspoons of papaya paste into each slot of an ice cube tray and freeze until firm. Transfer the cubes of papaya paste into sealable plastic bags, and return them to the freezer for future use. In general, use 2–3 ice cubes of green papaya for 2 pounds of meat.

VIETNAMESE-STYLE CHICKEN CURRY

Ca Ri Gà

YIELDS 6 SERVINGS

Ca Ri Gà is heavily inspired by Indian cuisine, with minor variations. The chicken is cooked in coconut milk with cashew nuts along with potatoes. Simply serve with *bánh mì* on the side so the bread can be dipped in the thin, spicy gravy.

2 green Thai chiles

1 (2") piece fresh ginger

2 pounds chicken drumsticks

2 teaspoons salt

¼ teaspoon ground cumin

½ teaspoon ground coriander

¾ teaspoon red chile powder, or to taste

½ teaspoon black pepper, freshly ground

2 cloves garlic, finely minced

1 teaspoon baking powder

¼ cup canola oil

¼ cup cashew nuts

1½ yellow onions, chopped

1 bay leaf

1 cinnamon stick, broken in half

2 teaspoons fresh curry leaves, torn in half

1 tablespoon green cardamom pods, crushed

½ teaspoon cloves

¼ teaspoon turmeric powder

1 teaspoon whole black peppercorns

2 carrots, peeled and cut into 3" pieces

½ cup water chestnuts, cooked and sliced

1 tablespoon grated palm sugar, to taste

2 tablespoons Thai basil leaves

2 (5.6-ounce) cans unsweetened coconut milk

½–1 cup water

3 Yukon Gold potatoes, boiled, skinned, and cut into quarters

1 teaspoon Fish Sauce (*Nước Mắm Chấm*; see Chapter 6)

6 baguettes

1. **Preparing the chiles:** Using a paring knife, cut a 2"–3" slit in the peppers. For less heat, remove the seeds (don't forget to wear disposable gloves).

2. **Preparing the ginger:** Clean the ginger, carefully removing any dirt. Peel the ginger root with a paring knife or the edge of a spoon, then grate about 2 tablespoons and finely chop the rest.

3. **Preparing the chicken:** Wash the chicken and pat it dry using paper towels. Gather the meat in a large mixing bowl. Season with salt, cumin, coriander, 1 teaspoon of red chile powder, and black pepper. Add 1 teaspoon minced garlic and the baking powder. Toss well. Drizzle with about 1 tablespoon of the oil. Marinate in the refrigerator for at least 2 hours.

4. **Preparing the cashew nuts:** Fill a small saucepan with water and bring to a boil. Blanch the cashews for 30 seconds; let sit for 2–3 minutes. Drain and coarsely chop.

5. **Preparing the gravy:** In a wok, heat the remaining oil. Add the onion and cook on high heat until slightly golden. Lower the heat to medium-low and continue cooking until soft and tender, about 6 minutes total. Transfer the mixture to a food processor, leaving as much oil in the wok as possible and blend until smooth. Set aside.

6. **Assembly time:** In the same wok, add the remaining garlic, bay leaf, cinnamon, and chopped ginger. Cook until slightly golden. Add the green chiles, curry leaves, cardamom, cloves, turmeric powder, whole peppercorns, and grated ginger. Add the chicken and sear the meat on all sides. Add the onion mixture, carrots, and water chestnuts; stir until the gravy becomes thick (about 30 seconds). Add palm sugar, Thai basil, coconut milk, and ½ cup water (up to 1 cup). Bring to a boil, then lower the heat to medium-low. Scrape the caramelized bits from the bottom of the wok with a wooden spoon. Add the potatoes. Reduce the liquid by cooking (uncovered) for about 10 minutes. Add the fish sauce and coarsely chopped cashews. Adjust seasoning of the gravy (if necessary) with salt and pepper. Bring to a boil one last time and cook until the gravy is thickened and the rest of the liquid has evaporated. Turn off the heat. Cover and let sit until you're ready to serve. Serve with bread for dipping on the side.

CHICKEN BOLOGNA SAUSAGE

Chả Lụa Gà Chiên

YIELDS 6 SERVINGS

Have you ever wondered how chicken bologna sausage is actually made? This recipe leads you through the few steps of how delicious Vietnamese-style bologna sausage is prepared. Plus, you will feel proud about making your own cold cuts!

2 tablespoons tapioca starch (or potato flour)
1 tablespoon grated palm sugar
1 tablespoon baking powder
2 tablespoons lukewarm water
1 tablespoon plus 1 teaspoon vegetable oil
2 shallots, finely chopped
2 pounds chicken (dark meat)
1 tablespoon Fish Sauce (*Nước Mắm Chấm*; see Chapter 6)
1 teaspoon white pepper, freshly ground
1 teaspoon mushroom seasoning salt (*bột nêm*) (or regular salt)
1 teaspoon whole white peppercorns
4 (10" × 10") frozen banana leaves, thawed
¾ teaspoon salt

1. **For the binding agent:** In a small bowl, combine the tapioca starch (or potato flour), sugar, and baking powder with lukewarm water. Stir well and let sit for 15 minutes.

2. **Cooking the shallots:** In small pan, heat 1 tablespoon oil. Add the shallots and cook for 2 minutes until softened over medium-low heat. Do not allow them to cook so much that they start to darken.

3. **Grinding the meat:** Dark meat (chicken thighs) is recommended for this dish; you could use chicken breast, but the dark meat will produce a juicy, moist, and flavorful bologna sausage. Before you start grinding the meat, be sure it's free of bones. Pass the meat through a meat grinder attachment. Add the tapioca mixture, shallots, fish sauce, white pepper, and mushroom seasoning salt. Mix well and refrigerate for at least 3 hours.

4. **Preparing the meat sausage:** Divide the meat mixture in half and blend in 2 batches in a food processor, adding 1–2 tablespoons water to make the blending easier. Transfer the meat mixture to a bowl, add the peppercorns, and mix well.

5. **Preparing the banana leaves:** Using a towel moistened in hot water, clean the leaves to soften them and to prevent tearing while rolling. Using a dry cloth, pat the leaves dry.

6. **Forming the sausage:** Place a large piece of plastic wrap on a flat surface. Top with 2 sheets of banana leaves, forming a long sheet, and layer one over the other by about 3"–4". Make sure the veins of the leaves are placed horizontally. Line the second layers in the same manner, but place the veins of the leaves vertically, on top of the horizontal leaves. Brush the leaves with a thin layer of oil. Wet your hands with warm water and spread the chicken mixture in the center of the leaves. Add a sprinkling of salt. Gather the top part of the leaves, and fold 3 times until you reach the center where the meat is placed. Gather the bottom part of the leaves, and fold 3 times until you reach the center. Tightly and slowly roll the leaves so the mixture forms a cylinder shape, and the folded parts overlap. Press gently with both hands for about 10 seconds, to ensure the sausage becomes firm. Secure and tie the roll, right in the center, with a small piece of string. Roughly fold one end of the cylinder and let it sit on its base. Even out and trim the top end with kitchen shears. Gently press the chicken mixture so it's tightly packed. Fold down the top flaps and flatten them against the

sausage. Make sure it's secured tightly; the sausage might be a bit on the thin side, but it will expand when cooked. Flip to the opposite end. Repeat the same trimming and folding procedure on the other end to seal. Secure and tie the roll by sliding a long piece of string underneath the sausage length-wise to seal both ends. Loop the string through the width-wise knot to secure. Make 3 tight knots, at equal distance, around the width of the sausage to secure. Trim the excess strings.

7. **Steaming the sausage:** Pour water in the bottom of a steamer to a depth of at least 3". Place the rack in the steamer. Bring the water to a boil, then lower the heat to medium-high. Place the roll in the steamer, cover, and steam for about 30–40 minutes. The roll should be tender but still firm. Remove from the steamer. Let cool a little. Chill in the refrigerator for at least 2 hours.

8. **Making *chả chiên* (frying the bologna sausage skin):** Remove and discard the strings. Unwrap the sausage and discard the banana leaves. In a small, nonstick pan, heat 1 teaspoon oil. Add the whole sausage and pan-fry over high heat for 2 minutes until golden brown. Transfer to a cutting board. Dip a very sharp kitchen knife in hot water and wipe it clean. Cut the roll into thick slices.

9. **Sandwich assembly:** Use 1 baguette per serving. Cut lengthwise into the baguette and remove some of the crumb. Spread a thin layer of softened butter on one side and driz-zle Maggi Seasoning on the other. Add the sliced *chả lụa* (sausage). Drizzle the inside of the baguette with Vegetar-ian Dipping Sauce (*Nước Chấm Chay*; see Chapter 6) and Sriracha hot sauce (to taste). Fill the sandwich with thin slices of jalapeño and the condiment(s) of your choice, such as Pickled Vietnamese Cabbage (*Dưa Muối*) and Pickled Carrots and Daikon (*Đồ Chua*) (see Chapter 6 for both con-diments). Garnish with 2 sprigs of cilantro. Close the sand-wich tightly.

TAPIOCA STARCH   Tapioca starch is a very common ingredient in Asian cooking. It's used as a filler for making bologna sausage. You can find it in any Asian specialty market. You can replace it with potato flour, which is available in the baking aisle of most traditional grocery stores.

SOY-ROASTED CORNISH HEN

Gà Mái Rô Ti

YIELDS 2 SERVINGS

Gà Mái was brought to Vietnam by the French, who called it a *coquelet*. It's a smaller hybrid chicken, also known as a Cornish game hen. But contrary to its name, it's not a game bird. The meat is very tender, and the dark, sweet, crispy skin is the best part.

2 whole hens with skin on, rinsed and patted dry, cut in half lengthwise (about 1–1½ pounds each)
2 tablespoons freshly ground green papaya with seeds
3 tablespoons plain yogurt
1 (2") piece fresh ginger
1 tablespoon honey
1 teaspoon baking powder
1 teaspoon five-spice powder
2 tablespoons soy sauce
5 cloves garlic, finely minced
2 tablespoons vegetable oil

TWO DAYS BEFORE SERVING:

1. **Preparing the birds:** Trim the fat around the bottom of the hens. Wash the birds and pat them dry with paper towels. Mix the papaya and the yogurt. Make long parallel cuts on the flesh of the hens using a sharp boning knife, 2 on the breast and 2 on the thighs. Cover the hens inside and out with yogurt and papaya mixture. Plastic wrap the hens on a plate and refrigerate overnight. The next day, rinse the hens and discard all the yogurt mixture. Pat dry.

ONE DAY BEFORE SERVING:

2. **Preparing the ginger:** Clean the ginger, peel it with a paring knife or the back of a spoon, and grate it.

3. **Marinating the meat:** Mix the ginger, honey, baking powder, five-spice powder, soy sauce, minced garlic, and vegetable oil in a bowl. Reserve 2 tablespoons for basting. Spread ¾ of the mixture under the skin, in the cavity, and on the outside of the birds. Rub evenly. Place the birds in a dish, seal with plastic wrap, and refrigerate overnight.

SERVING DAY:

4. **Roasting the hens:** Remove the birds from the refrigerator 15 minutes in advance of cooking so the meat is at room temperature. Preheat the oven to 400°F. Grease the grill of a roasting pan with oil and place a shallow dish at the bottom to collect the drippings from the birds. Place the hens in the roasting pan on the middle rack of the oven, skin side up. Bake for 15–20 minutes per pound of poultry. At the end, brush the birds with the reserved marinade using a silicone brush, change the oven setting, and broil for 3 minutes. Immediately remove from the oven. Loosely cover with aluminum foil so the skin remains crispy. Let sit for 15 minutes before carving. A meat thermometer should register 165°F in the thickest part of the bird or the juices should run clear when you wiggle one of the thighs.

5. **Sandwich assembly:** Bone the hens and cut them into large pieces. Use 1 baguette per serving. Cut lengthwise into the baguette and remove some of the crumb. Spread a thin layer of softened butter on one side and Lime Mayonnaise (*Sốt Ma Dô Ne*; see Chapter 6) on the other. Add the poultry. Fill the sandwich with thin slices of jalapeño, *xà lách son* (Vietnamese watercress), seeded tomato wedges, and the condiment(s) of your choice, such as Pickled Bean Sprouts (*Dưa Giá Với Hẹ Trái Táo Xanh*) and Pickled Carrots and Daikon (*Đồ Chua*) (see Chapter 6 for both condiments). Garnish with 2 sprigs of cilantro. Close the sandwich tightly.

VIETNAMESE GINGER CHICKEN

Gà Kho Gừng

YIELDS 6 SERVINGS

Tender, ginger-flavored chicken is the filling for this sandwich. The natural amber color from the fish sauce, along with ginger and curry powder (specifically, the turmeric), make a flavorful and appealing dish.

1½ cups water

1 red Thai bird chile

1½ pounds chicken thighs, chopped into small pieces

2 lemons, freshly squeezed

¾ teaspoon black pepper

4 tablespoons canola oil (or any neutral oil)

2 cloves garlic, crushed and finely minced

1 (3") chunk fresh ginger, peeled and finely shredded

3 tablespoons fish sauce, to taste

¾ teaspoon curry powder

1½ cups hot water

1. **Preparing the water and chile:** Fill a saucepan with water and bring to a boil. Using a paring knife, cut a deep slit in the red Thai chile. For less heat, remove the seeds (don't forget to wear disposable gloves). Cut it in half diagonally. Set aside.

2. **Preparing the chicken:** Wash the chicken and drizzle with lemon juice. Let sit for 15 minutes, then pat dry using paper towels. There should be as little moisture as possible. Season the chicken with ¼ teaspoon black pepper. Drizzle with about 1 tablespoon of oil.

3. **Assembly time:** Heat 2 tablespoons of canola oil in a wok that has a matching lid. Once the oil is hot, add the garlic and 2 tablespoons of shredded ginger and cook for 1–2 minutes until fragrant. Add the pieces of chicken. Sear the meat for 2–3 minutes on all sides. Add the red chile pepper and cook for an additional minute. Season with

2 tablespoons fish sauce and the curry powder. Stir well, then cover with the hot water. The liquid should barely cover the chicken. Bring to a boil, then lower the heat to a gentle simmer. Keep stirring often until the chicken is fully cooked. Once the liquid is almost reduced, check the doneness of the meat (add another ½ cup of water and cook a bit longer if not fully cooked). Adjust seasoning with more fish sauce. There should be caramel-colored gravy at the bottom of the pan. Add ½ teaspoon black pepper and the remaining ginger. Toss well. Cover with wok lid until ready to serve. Remove and discard the pieces of red chile.

4. **Sandwich assembly:** Use 1 baguette per serving. Cut lengthwise into the baguette and remove some of the crumb. Spread a thin layer of butter on one side and Lime Mayonnaise (*Sốt Ma Dô Ne*; see Chapter 6) on the other. Add the ginger chicken. Fill the sandwich with thin slices of jalapeño, Thai basil leaves, and the condiment(s) of your choice, such as Beet Pickles (*Củ Cải Đường Muối Chua*) and Pickled Carrots and Daikon (*Đồ Chua*) (see Chapter 6 for both condiments). Garnish with 2 sprigs of cilantro. Close the sandwich tightly.

USING DARK MEAT VERSUS CHICKEN BREAST Chicken thighs have a higher fat content than white meat. The result will be a more moist and flavorful dish. You could also mix 1 part chicken breast to 1 part chicken thigh, if you prefer white meat.

SOY GINGER QUAIL

Chim Cút Rô Ti

YIELDS 6 SERVINGS

There are many Vietnamese versions of French dishes. In this dish, a sweet ginger glaze made of honey, red chile powder, ginger, and soy sauce replaces the mustard, coriander, and white wine typically found in the French version.

1 teaspoon black peppercorns

1 (3") chunk fresh ginger, peeled and freshly grated

1 teaspoon ground coriander

¼ teaspoon baking powder

1 tablespoon freshly grated green papaya with its seeds (see sidebar in Chicken Teriyaki recipe, Chapter 3)

½ teaspoon red chile powder

1 lemon, freshly squeezed

4 tablespoons canola oil

6 quail

1 cup dark soy sauce

2 cloves garlic, finely minced

2½ tablespoons honey

½ cup green onions, cut into 2" pieces

½ cup water

xà lách son (Vietnamese watercress), to taste

1. **For the marinade:** In a mortar and pestle, grind ½ teaspoon peppercorns. Add ginger, ground coriander, baking powder, papaya paste, red chile powder, 2 tablespoons lemon juice, and 1 tablespoon of the oil. Mix until well combined.

2. **Preparing the meat:** Clean the quail and pat them dry with paper towels. Cut them in half vertically using sharp poultry shears. Coat them with the contents from the mortar and pestle. Let marinate for at least 1 hour in the refrigerator.

3. **Seasoning the meat:** Pour the soy sauce into a small bowl. The soy sauce should reach a depth of at least 2"; if it doesn't, use a smaller bowl. Add half of minced garlic, honey, and ½ teaspoon freshly cracked pepper. Add the quail; let rest for at least 30 minutes.

4. **Cooking the quail:** Heat the rest of the oil in a wok. Place the quail skin side down (with as little marinade as possible); add the remaining garlic and the green onions. Brown the skin for 2 minutes. Lower the heat to medium-high and cook the quail on the other side for another 2 minutes. Flip again. Add half the amount of the marinade and water, then bring to a boil. Boil the other half in a small saucepan. Cook the quail for 8 minutes until the liquid is reduced to half. Add the remaining lemon juice. Baste the quail with the saucepan marinade. Cover and cook for another 2 minutes.

5. **Sandwich assembly:** Bone the quail and cut the meat into large pieces. Use 1 baguette per serving. Cut lengthwise into the baguette and remove some of the crumb. Spread a thin layer of softened butter on one side and Lime Mayonnaise (*Sốt Ma Dô Ne*; see Chapter 6) on the other. Add the ginger quail. Fill the sandwich with thinly sliced jalapeño, *xà lách son*, Thai basil leaves, and the condiment(s) of your choice, such as Pickled Papaya (*Gỏi Đu Đủ*) and Pickled Carrots and Daikon (*Đồ Chua*) (see Chapter 6 for both condiments). Garnish with 2 sprigs of cilantro. Close the sandwich tightly.

SOY GINGER QUAIL: *Chim Cút Rô Ti*

PÂTÉ

Ba Tê Gan Xay

YIELDS 2½ CUPS

Gan Xay is pâté, a Cognac-accented spreadable paste. Chicken livers, onions, bay leaves (*lá nguyệt quể*), dry sherry (*rượu trắng*), and a generous amount of butter are blended to form a perfect spread for a *bánh mì*.

1 pound chicken livers
1 tablespoon white vinegar
1 cup milk
2 tablespoons vegetable oil
3 cloves garlic, finely minced
4 tablespoons butter
2 shallots, finely chopped
½ white onion
2 bay leaves
2 teaspoons salt
1 teaspoon white pepper, freshly ground
1 teaspoon granulated sugar
¼ cup dry sherry
½ cup water
1 tablespoon cognac (or brandy)
1 cup unsalted butter, softened to room temperature
¼ cup heavy cream
⅛ teaspoon red chile powder
⅛ teaspoon black pepper, coarsely ground

1. **Preparing the livers:** Remove and discard the white membrane and trim any fatty residue on each piece of liver; it's chewy and unpleasant. Place the livers in a bowl and barely cover with salted water and white vinegar. Soak for 5 minutes. Rinse livers, transfer to a new bowl, and add milk. Mix well and refrigerate for 30 minutes. Drain, leaving as little milk as possible, but do not rinse.

2. **Cooking the livers:** Heat the oil in a wok. Once it's hot, add the garlic and cook for 1 minute. Add 4 tablespoons butter, the shallots, onions, and bay leaves. Cook for 4 minutes until fragrant. Add the chicken livers, 1 teaspoon of the salt, white pepper, sugar, dry sherry, and water. Stir well and bring to a boil. Cook for 3 minutes until the meat changes color; don't overcook the livers. Add cognac; stir and cook for another 2 minutes. Turn off the heat, cover, and let sit for 10 minutes. Remove and discard the bay leaves.

3. **Forming a paste:** Using a slotted spoon, transfer the livers, onions, and shallots to a food processor, discarding the liquid. Adding a few tablespoons of softened butter at a time, pulse the liver mixture until smooth, adding ¾ cup butter total. Add the heavy cream and blend until creamy and firm.

4. **Assembly time:** Melt the remaining butter. Lightly butter the insides of 3 mini casserole dishes. Divide and pour the liver mixture into the containers. Seal the top with a thin layer of melted butter. Sprinkle with black pepper. Plastic-wrap the containers and chill in the refrigerator for at least 4 hours until hardened, preferably overnight. The containers should be tightly sealed, because otherwise the fat from the butter may pick up some other food odor from the refrigerator.

5. **Sandwich assembly:** Remove the pâté from the refrigerator 15 minutes ahead of time so it's not too stiff. Use 1 baguette per serving. Cut lengthwise into the baguette and remove some of the crumb. Spread a layer of pâté on one side and Lime Mayonnaise (*Sốt Ma Dô Ne*; see Chapter 6) on the other. Arrange thinly sliced Vietnamese-Style Cold Cuts (*Thịt Nguội*; see Chapter 4). Add sliced *chả lụa* of your choice: Vegetarian Bologna Sausage (*Chả Lụa Chay*), Chapter 2; Chicken Bologna Sausage (*Chả Lụa Gà Chiên*), Chapter 3; or Steamed Ham Roll (*Chả Lụa Bì*), Chapter 4. Add sliced jalapeño pepper, a few pieces of cucumber, and the condiment(s) of your choice, such as Pickled Carrots and Daikon (*Đồ Chua*; see Chapter 6). Garnish with 2 sprigs of cilantro. Close the sandwich tightly. You can store the pâté for up to 10 days in the refrigerator or up to 3 months in the freezer.

PÂTÉ: *Ba Tê Gan Xay*

CHAPTER 4

MEAT SANDWICHES

When you think about *bánh mì* sandwiches, beef (*thịt bò*) and pork (*thịt heo*) probably come to mind the most. If you walk into any *bánh mì* shop, you'll see several combinations of beef and pork products featured in the sandwiches. Once you learn the recipes in this section, you'll be able to create your own blends, and mix and match your favorite meats. If you're pressed for time, consider making the meat portion of the recipe the night before and serving it for dinner. Then use the leftovers in your sandwich the next day. In addition, feel free to replace the listed meat with your favorite alternatives, such as turkey (*thịt gà lôi*), veal (*thịt bò con*), or even lamb (*thịt dê*).

The recipes in this chapter are for typical meat *bánh mì* fillings, ones you would find in a *bánh mì* shop. In general, use 1 small authentic Vietnamese baguette per serving, or ⅓ of a larger French baguette. (Try making your own! See the Vietnamese Baguette: *Bánh Mì Baguette* recipe in Chapter 1.) For each recipe, the final step includes sandwich assembly instructions. You can choose to use the suggested ingredients, or mix and match your favorite flavors to taste. The listed ingredients are a general guide, and you can customize your sandwiches for a unique *bánh mì* experience every time.

VIETNAMESE BEEF SALAD

Xà Lách Thit Bò

YIELDS 6 SERVINGS

Perfectly juicy steak is served thinly sliced at room temperature with *xà lách son*, or Vietnamese watercress. *Xà lách son* is a typical Asian herb with a very distinctive flavor, similar to French *mâche* leaves. The marinade consists of a standard fish sauce mixture, very common in Vietnamese cuisine.

2 shallots, thinly sliced

1 (2") piece fresh ginger, peeled and finely diced

Juice of 1 lime, freshly squeezed

2 tablespoons Chinese brown sugar (*đường thẻ*) (or regular brown sugar)

4 tablespoons vegetable oil

1 teaspoon salt

½ teaspoon black pepper, coarsely ground

¾ teaspoon baking powder

1 teaspoon cayenne powder

2 teaspoons mushroom seasoning salt (*bột nêm*) (or regular salt)

3 (10-ounce) rib-eye steaks, or your favorite cut

⅓ cup soy sauce

1 tablespoon Fish Sauce (*Nước Mắm Chấm*; see Chapter 6), plus more for garnish

2 green Thai chiles, seeded, finely chopped

2 green onions, cut into 2" pieces diagonally

2 cloves garlic, finely minced

1 (16-ounce) bunch *xà lách son* (Vietnamese watercress)

1. **Pickling the shallots:** In a small bowl, drizzle the shallots with ½ teaspoon grated ginger, 1 tablespoon lime juice, 1 teaspoon of the brown sugar, and 1 tablespoon of the oil. Season with salt and pepper. Mix well and set aside.

2. **Preparing the meat:** In a small bowl, combine baking powder, cayenne powder, and 2 teaspoons mushroom seasoning salt. Gently dry the pieces of meat using paper towels. Rub the meat with this dry mixture. Set aside for 15 minutes.

3. **Cooking the meat:** In a small bowl, combine the soy sauce, 1 tablespoon fish sauce, remaining brown sugar, remaining lime juice, and green chiles. Stir well. In a large pan, heat the remaining vegetable oil. Add the green onions. Cook for 2 minutes until softened and fragrant. Transfer to a bowl, leaving about 2–3 tablespoons of oil in the pan. In the same pan, fry the garlic until golden. Add the remaining grated ginger and cook for 1 minute until fragrant but not browned. Add the pieces of meat and sear one side for 2–3 minutes. Once an outer crust is formed, flip the meat and sear the other side for 2–3 minutes. Add the dark soy sauce mixture, lower the heat to medium-low, and cook for 2–3 more minutes, flipping the pieces of meat periodically until the liquid thickens.

4. **Assembly time:** Once the meat is cooked, turn off the heat; add the pickled shallots and grilled onions. Toss well until evenly distributed and let rest on the stove for 2–3 minutes before removing to a plate. Cover with a piece of aluminum foil and let cool to room temperature (at least 10 minutes) before slicing. Slice thin on the bias (against the grain, so the meat will be tender) and transfer the beef to a bed of greens (*xà lách son*). Toss well and immediately transfer to a sandwich so the greens remain crisp.

5. **Sandwich assembly:** Use 1 baguette per serving. Cut lengthwise into the baguette and remove some of the crumb. Spread a thin layer of softened butter on one side and Lime Mayonnaise (*Sốt Ma Dô Ne*; see Chapter 6) on the other. Fill with *xà lách son*. Arrange slices of beef, shallots, and onions on top. Drizzle with *nước mắm chấm*. Add thinly sliced jalapeño pepper and the condiment(s) of your choice, such as Pickled Asparagus (*Gỏi Măng Tây*) and Pickled Carrots and Daikon (*Đồ Chua*) (see Chapter 6 for both condiments). Garnish with 2 sprigs of cilantro. Close the sandwich tightly.

VIETNAMESE-STYLE BEEF CARPACCIO

Bò Tái Chanh

YIELDS 4 SERVINGS

Bò Tái Chanh is the equivalent of Western carpaccio. Very thinly sliced, fresh, raw beef sirloin is prepared with lime juice and embellished with red bell peppers, pineapple, onions, chiles, and peanuts. It's considered a dish for a *tiệc* (feast); it is indeed a "rare" treat!

2 red Thai chile peppers (to taste), stemmed and finely chopped

7 limes

3 tablespoons granulated sugar

2 tablespoons vegetable oil

2 shallots, thinly sliced

1½ white onions, sliced

1 teaspoon salt

¼ cup red bell peppers, thinly sliced and cut into 2" long pieces

2 teaspoons white vinegar

2 pounds flank steak, or your favorite cut (filet mignon guarantees optimum tenderness)

1 teaspoon black pepper, freshly ground

1 fresh pineapple, peeled and cored

1 quart water

1 green onion (green part only), for garnish

3 tablespoons hoisin sauce

1 tablespoon Sriracha hot sauce

3 cloves Pickled Garlic (*Tỏi Chua Ngọt*; see Chapter 6), thinly sliced

2 jalapeño peppers, stemmed and thinly sliced

1 tablespoon Fish Sauce (*Nước Mắm Chấm*; see Chapter 6), plus more for garnish

1 cup *rau răm* (Vietnamese coriander)

1 cup Vietnamese mint

1 cup Thai basil

½ cup cilantro

2 tablespoons roasted peanuts, coarsely chopped, plus more for garnish

1. **Preparing the chiles:** Stem the chiles. Using a paring knife, cut a 2"–3" slit in the peppers. Remove some of the seeds (to reduce heat) and finely chop. Place in a mortar and pestle and mash into a coarse paste.

2. **Preparing the limes:** Juice 5 limes and add 2 tablespoons of the sugar. Cut the remaining limes into small wedges.

3. **Frying the shallots:** Heat the oil in a large nonstick pan. Add the shallots and fry for 6–7 minutes until golden brown. Transfer to a plate, lined with paper towels. Reserve 1 tablespoon of the oil.

4. **Preparing the onions:** Place the sliced onions in a large bowl. Sprinkle with salt. Let sit for 1 hour. Press out and drain. Rinse in a water bath, then drain again and pat dry. Add the red bell peppers, 2 teaspoons of the sugar, and vinegar. Toss well.

5. **Preparing the meat:** Place the beef in the freezer for at least 1 hour. Then thinly slice the meat (as thin as possible, about ⅛"-thick) using a sharp chef's knife. Make sure to cut the meat across the grain. Season with pepper, add half the chiles, and mix well. Spread the thin slices in a large colander (working in batches).

6. **Preparing the pineapple and beef:** Coarsely chop the pineapple and the remaining red chiles and transfer to a blender. Add 1 quart water and blend until smooth. Transfer to a saucepan with a spout (to be able to control the flow of liquid) and bring to a boil. Slowly pour the hot liquid over the beef in the colander so it barely changes color while remaining rare. Transfer the beef to a serving platter and repeat until all the beef lightly changes color. Squeeze the beef and remove as much liquid as possible. Pat dry and transfer the meat to a large mixing bowl. Add the lime juice; mix well and let sit for 20 minutes. Drain and squeeze as much liquid as possible and pat dry.

7. **For the green onion garnish:** Cut the green onion into 3"-pieces. On one end make several small lengthwise cuts using a paring knife. Repeat the same procedure on the other end, leaving about ½" in between. Transfer to ice water.

8. **Assembly time:** Add hoisin sauce, Sriracha sauce, the reserved shallot-flavored oil, pickled garlic, sliced jalapeño peppers, and 1 tablespoon *nước mắm chấm* to the beef. Mix

well until coated uniformly. Add the *rau răm*, mint, basil, and cilantro. Toss well. Transfer to a platter. Top with fried shallots and 2 tablespoons peanuts. Garnish with green onion curls.

9. **Sandwich assembly:** Use 1 baguette per serving. Cut lengthwise into the baguette and remove some of the crumb. Spread a thin layer of softened butter on one side and Lime Mayonnaise (*Sốt Ma Dô Ne*; see Chapter 6) on the other. Fill with beef carpaccio. Add crushed *bánh phồng tôm* (Vietnamese shrimp chips) for added crunch. Drizzle with *nước mắm chấm*. Add the condiment(s) of your choice, such as Pickled Mango (*Gỏi Xoài Xanh*; see Chapter 6). Garnish with more peanuts, fried shallots, and 2 sprigs of cilantro. Close the sandwich tightly. Serve with wedges of lime on the side.

VIETNAMESE-STYLE COLD CUTS

Thịt Nguội

YIELDS 6 SERVINGS

Thịt Nguội literally translates to "meat that has turned cold." Customarily, *Thịt Nguội* is made with pork belly and is seasoned with cloves, garlic, ginger, and soy sauce. It gets its name from the fact that it is stored in an ice box or refrigerator and is served cold. The skin is colored red to give it a more appealing look, and the meat is thinly sliced before serving. It's a mildly flavored luncheon meat that makes a perfect canvas upon which to layer condiments, pickles, and even other cold cuts.

1¼ pounds *thịt ba rọi* (pork belly, similar to pancetta)
3 drops red food coloring (optional)
2 tablespoons honey
3 cloves, freshly ground
1 teaspoon salt
3 cloves garlic, freshly grated
1 teaspoon garlic powder
¼ teaspoon red chile powder
2 teaspoons ginger, freshly grated
1 tablespoon brown sugar
3 tablespoons soy sauce
½ cup water

1. **Preparing the meat:** Choose a piece of meat at least 1½" thick, with a thin layer of fat. Wearing disposable gloves, spread 2 drops of food coloring (if using) on the side where the layer of fat is located. Spread and distribute the food coloring onto the fatty layer. Place in a sealable zip-top bag.

2. **For the marinade:** In a small bowl, combine the honey, cloves, salt, garlic, garlic powder, red chile powder, ginger, brown sugar, and soy sauce. Add 1 drop red food coloring (if using) and water. Stir well.

3. **Marinating the meat:** Cover the meat with the marinade in the bag. Make sure the meat is well coated. Seal the bag, place in a shallow baking dish, and refrigerate for at least 4 hours, preferably overnight.

4. **Securing the meat:** Line a flat surface with plastic wrap (so it doesn't get stained), and place the meat on top, fat side down. Pat the meat dry and roll it into a large cylinder, with the fat layer on the outside. Tie a thick strip of plastic wrap in the center of the pork roll (parallel to the ends) to temporarily tighten it. Cut a piece of twine or string long enough to tie around the roll, as with the plastic wrap. Place the twine underneath the roll, bring the ends up, cross them over twice, then pull the string tight and make a knot. Repeat 2 more times along the length of the roll. Snip and discard the temporary tie made with the plastic wrap. Securing the roll in this way gives it a more compact shape, which allows the meat to cook more uniformly and ensures a better presentation.

5. **Cooking the roll:** Pour water in the bottom of a steamer to a depth of at least 3". Place the rack in the steamer. Bring the water to a boil, then lower the heat to medium-high. Place the roll in the steamer; cover and steam for 80–90 minutes, adding more water if necessary. The roll should be firm. Remove from the steamer. Let cool to room temperature, and then chill the roll in the refrigerator for at least 4 hours, preferably overnight. Once chilled (the colder it is, the easier to carve), remove and discard the twine. Transfer the roll to a cutting board and cut into slices as thin as possible.

6. **Sandwich assembly:** Use 1 baguette per serving. Cut lengthwise into the baguette and remove some of the crumb. Spread a layer of Pâté (*Ba Tê Gan Xay*; see Chapter 3) on one side and Lime Mayonnaise (*Sốt Ma Dô Ne*; see Chapter 6) on the other. Arrange the thinly sliced meat roll (*thịt nguội*), and sliced *chả lụa* of your choice: Vegetarian Bologna Sausage (*Chả Lụa Chay*), Chapter 2; Chicken Bologna Sausage (*Chả Lụa Gà Chiên)*, Chapter 3; or Steamed Ham Roll (*Chả Lụa Bì*), Chapter 4. Add sliced jalapeño pepper, a few pieces of cucumber, and the condiment(s) of your choice, such as Pickled Carrots and Daikon (*Đô Chua*; see Chapter 6). Garnish with 2 sprigs of cilantro. Close the sandwich tightly. (Note: You can store the *thịt nguội* in the refrigerator for up to 1 week.)

STEAMED HAM ROLL

Chả Lụa Bì

YIELDS 6 SERVINGS

Chả Lụa Bì is another kind of *chả lụa* bologna sausage made with pork and pork skin (*bì*). *Giò Bì* has crunchy bits and is similar to French andouille sausage because of the addition of *couenne* (pork rind).

2 tablespoons tapioca starch
1 tablespoon grated palm sugar (or potato starch)
1 teaspoon baking soda
1½ teaspoons baking powder
2 tablespoons lukewarm water
½ (1-pound) package frozen cooked sliced pork skin, thawed
1 tablespoon vegetable oil
1 white onion, finely chopped
 1½ pounds pork butt, freshly ground
1 tablespoon Fish Sauce (*Nước Mắm Chấm*; see Chapter 6)
1 teaspoon white pepper, freshly ground
1 teaspoon mushroom seasoning salt (*bột nêm*) (or regular salt)
1 teaspoon whole white peppercorns
4 (10" × 10") frozen banana leaves, thawed

1. **For the binding agent:** In a small bowl, combine the tapioca starch, sugar (or potato starch), baking soda, baking powder, and lukewarm water. Stir well and let sit for 15 minutes.

2. **Preparing the pork skin:** Place the thawed pork skin in lukewarm salted water. Cover and let sit for 30 minutes. Stir every now and then so it doesn't form a block. Drain thoroughly and pat dry, removing as much liquid as possible. Cut into 2"–3"-long strips.

3. **Cooking the onions:** Heat the oil in small pan. Add the onion and cook for 3 minutes until softened but not browned.

4. **Grinding the meat:** Pass the meat through a meat grinder or a food processor. Add the binding agent mixture, cooked onions, fish sauce, ground white pepper, and mushroom seasoning salt. Mix well and refrigerate for at least 3 hours.

5. **Preparing the meat sausage:** Divide the meat and blend in 2 batches in a food processor, adding 1–2 tablespoons of cold water for a smoother flow. Remove from the machine, add the pork skin and whole peppercorns, and mix well.

6. **Preparing the banana leaves:** Using a towel moistened in hot water, clean the banana leaves to soften them and to prevent tearing while rolling. Gently pat the damp leaves with a cloth to dry them.

7. **Forming the sausage:** Place a large piece of plastic wrap on a flat surface. Top with 2 sheets of banana leaves, forming a long sheet, and layer one over the other by about 3"–4". Make sure the veins of the leaves are placed horizontally. Line the second layers in the same manner, but place the veins of the leaves vertically, on top of the horizontal leaves. Brush the leaves with a thin layer of oil. Wet your hands with warm water and spread the meat mixture in the center of the leaves. Gather the top part of the leaves, and fold 3 times until you reach the center where the meat is placed. Gather the bottom part of the leaves, and fold 3 times until you reach the center. Tightly and slowly roll the leaves so the mixture forms a cylinder shape, and the folded parts overlap. Press gently with both hands for about 10 seconds, to ensure the sausage becomes firm. Secure and tie the roll in the center with a small piece of string. Roughly fold one end of the cylinder and let it sit on its base. Even out and trim the top end with kitchen shears. Gently press the meat mixture so it's tightly packed. Fold down the top flaps and flatten them against the sausage. Make sure it's secured tightly; the sausage might be a bit on the thin side but it will expand when cooked. Flip to the opposite end. Repeat the same trimming and folding procedure on the other end to seal. Secure and tie the roll by sliding a long piece of string underneath the sausage lengthwise to seal both ends. Loop the string through the widthwise knot to secure. Make 3 tight knots, at equal distance, around the width of the sausage to secure. Trim the excess strings.

8. **Steaming the sausage:** Pour water in the bottom of a steamer to a depth of at least 3". Place the rack in the steamer. Bring the water to a boil, then lower the heat to medium-high. Place the roll in the steamer. Cover and steam for about 30–40 minutes. The roll should be tender but still firm. Remove from the steamer. Let cool a little. Chill in the refrigerator for at least 2 hours. Remove and discard the strings. Transfer to a cutting board. Dip a very sharp kitchen knife in hot water and wipe it clean. Cut the rolls in thick slices. Discard the banana leaves.

9. **Sandwich assembly:** Use 1 baguette per serving. Cut lengthwise into the baguette and remove some of the crumb. Spread a thin layer of butter on one side and drizzle Maggi Seasoning on the other. Add the sliced *chả bì*. Drizzle the inside of the baguette with Vegetarian Dipping Sauce (*Nước Chấm Chay*; see Chapter 6) and Sriracha hot sauce (to taste). Fill the sandwich with thin slices of jalapeño and the condiment(s) of your choice, such as Pickled Carrots and Daikon (*Đồ Chua*; see Chapter 6). Garnish with 2 sprigs of cilantro. Close the sandwich tightly.

CHAR SIU BARBECUE PORK

Thịt Xá Xíu

YIELDS 6 SERVINGS

The meat lovers in your life will love *xá xíu* (*char siu*), a flavorful barbecued pork glistening in red sauce. The sweet sauce is typically made with an acidic fruit pulp, sweeteners (honey), oyster sauce, dark soy sauce, dry sherry (optional), fresh ginger, five-spice powder, and sesame oil. A little red food coloring could be added to achieve the typical *char siu* color, but it's optional according to your taste.

2 pounds pork butt (or pork shoulder)

1 teaspoon garlic powder

¼ teaspoon red chile powder

1 teaspoon baking powder

2 teaspoons mushroom seasoning salt (*bột nêm*) (or regular salt)

¼ cup honey

⅓ cup oyster sauce (*dầu hào*)

1½ teaspoons five-spice powder

2 tablespoons black bean garlic sauce

2 slices canned pineapple (or other fruit such as orange, mango, kiwi, or pomegranate)

2 tablespoons chopped white onion

1 tablespoon ketchup

2 tablespoons dry sherry (*rượu gạo nấu ăn*) (optional)

2 teaspoons ginger, freshly grated

3 cloves garlic, freshly grated

2 tablespoons Chinese brown sugar (*đường thẻ*) (or regular brown sugar)

½ cup dark soy sauce

1–2 tablespoons water

2 drops red food coloring (optional)

3 tablespoons vegetable oil (or any neutral oil)

1 teaspoon sesame oil

½ teaspoon black pepper, coarsely ground

1. **Preparing the meat:** Slice the meat lengthwise into about 3"-thick slices (4 slices). In a small bowl, combine garlic powder, red chile powder, baking powder, and 1½ teaspoons mushroom seasoning salt. Gently dry the pieces of meat using paper towels. Rub the meat with the dry rub. Set aside for 15 minutes.

2. **For the *char siu* sauce:** In a blender, combine the honey, oyster sauce, five-spice powder, black bean garlic sauce, the pineapple, onions, ketchup, dry sherry (if using), ginger, garlic, brown sugar, and soy sauce. Add 1–2 tablespoons water for easier blending. Add red food coloring (if using). Mix well.

3. **Marinating the meat:** Place the pieces of meat in a large zip-top sealable bag. Cover with ¾ of the *char siu* sauce, reserving the rest for basting later. Make sure the meat is well coated. Seal the bag, place in a shallow baking dish, and refrigerate for at least 4 hours, preferably overnight.

4. **Cooking the meat:** Preheat the oven to 375°F. Heat the oil in a cast-iron skillet grill. Once the oil is really hot, almost to the smoking point, place the meat (with as little marinade as possible) on the grill with tongs and sear it for 2–3 minutes. Flip the meat and grill for another 3 minutes. Baste with the reserved *char siu* marinade; the pork should be generously coated with sauce. Transfer to the oven and cook for 20 minutes, basting the meat with more sauce every 10 minutes or so. Flip the meat, baste with more sauce, and continue cooking 10–15 more minutes. At the end of that time, switch to the oven's broiler setting and broil the meat for 2 minutes. Remove from the oven. Sprinkle with ½ teaspoon mushroom seasoning salt. Drizzle with sesame oil, lightly cover with aluminum foil, and allow to rest for at least 15 minutes before serving. Cut meat crosswise into thick slices, baste with more sauce from the drippings of the skillet, ensuring slices are all well covered. Sprinkle with black pepper.

5. **Sandwich assembly:** Use 1 baguette per serving. Cut lengthwise into the baguette and remove some of the crumb. Spread a thin layer of softened butter on one side. Add the sliced pork. Drizzle with Fish Sauce (*Nước Mắm Chấm*; see Chapter 6). Fill the sandwich with thin slices of jalapeño and the condiment(s) of your choice, such as Pickled Carrots and Daikon (*Đồ Chua*; see Chapter 6). Garnish with 2 sprigs of cilantro. Close the sandwich tightly.

GRILLED VIETNAMESE KEBABS

Nem Nướng

YIELDS 4 SERVINGS (8 PATTIES)

Nem Nướng are perfect for barbecue parties. They don't require a lot of work, so you don't have to end up slaving in the kitchen while your guests mingle. Once the meat kebabs are grilled, pair them with fresh cucumbers, carrots, bean sprouts, Vietnamese mint, *hẹ* (Chinese chives), and crunchy peanuts in a baguette. With this dish, your guests will be able to enjoy both your company *and* your food!

½ white onion, chopped

10 cloves garlic, finely minced

4½ tablespoons water

1½ pounds pork, freshly ground

½ pound turkey, freshly ground (or 2 pounds ground pork total)

1 tablespoon baking powder

1 tablespoon cornstarch

½ cup sugar

½ teaspoon red chile powder

1 tablespoon dry-roasted rice powder (see *Bì Chay* recipe, Chapter 2)

1 drop red food coloring (optional)

1 teaspoon mushroom seasoning salt (*bột nêm*) (or regular salt)

1 teaspoon salt

1½ teaspoons black pepper, coarsely ground

2 tablespoons vegetable oil, as needed

1 tablespoon honey, warmed (optional)

1. **Soaking the skewers:** While preparing the kebabs, soak bamboo skewers in water (for at least 30 minutes). This step will prevent the bamboo from burning on the grill. You could also use nonstick metal skewers.

2. **Flavoring the meat:** Place the chopped onions and garlic in a food processor. Add 2 tablespoons water and blend until smooth. Add the ground pork and turkey and pulse until well combined. Transfer to a mixing bowl.

3. **For the dry ingredients:** In a small bowl, dissolve the baking powder and cornstarch in 2 tablespoons water. Stir well and set aside.

4. **Seasoning the meat:** In a small saucepan, dissolve 2 tablespoons sugar with ½ teaspoon water. Stir gently by swirling the pan. Bring to a full boil, then lower heat to medium-low. As soon as the sugar caramelizes (turns golden brown), add the meat mixture. Mix well. Add red chile powder, rice powder, red food coloring (if using), the remaining sugar, and the cornstarch/baking powder mixture. Mix until well incorporated. Season with mushroom seasoning salt, salt, and pepper. Mix well. Cover with plastic wrap and refrigerate for at least 2 hours.

5. **Key to proper seasoning:** In a small pan, heat about 1 teaspoon of oil. Add 1 tablespoon of the meat mixture. Cook for 3 minutes. Taste the meat. Season with more sugar, salt, and pepper if necessary.

6. **Shaping the *nem nướng*:** Divide the meat mixture into 8 equal portions. Grease your hands with a little oil and form 6"-long kebabs around bamboo skewers. Flatten the kebabs to about ½"-thick. Brush them with a thin layer of oil.

7. **Assembly time:** Lightly and carefully brush the barbecue grill with oil, and then heat the grill to the hottest setting. Arrange the kebabs on the hot grill. Cook for 4–5 minutes on each side until grill marks are visible. Remove from the grill and transfer to a platter. Immediately brush the kebabs with a thin layer of honey (if using). The kebabs should have a dry crust on the outside and still be very moist on the inside.

8. **Sandwich assembly:** Use 1 baguette per serving. Cut lengthwise into the baguette and remove some of the crumb. Spread a thin layer of softened butter on one side. Add 2 patties per sandwich. Add sliced cucumber, 1 *hẹ* leaf (Chinese chives), chopped Vietnamese mint leaves, and the condiments of your choice, such as Pickled Carrots and Daikon (*Đồ Chua*) and Pickled Bean Sprouts (*Dưa Giá Với Hẹ Trái Táo Xanh*) (see Chapter 6 for both condiments). Sprinkle coarsely chopped salted peanuts on top. Close the sandwich tightly.

BEEF JERKY AND PAPAYA SALAD

Gỏi Đu Đủ Khô Bò

YIELDS 6 SERVINGS

Vietnamese beef jerky is very addictive. Although the meat is sufficiently preserved and dried to allow safe storage at room temperature, the texture remains malleable enough to shred into pieces to fill a sandwich. Salt is the key ingredient; it draws out moisture and preserves the beef for long storage. However, this jerky is so good that it won't last long, especially when it's paired with pickled papaya.

4 red Thai chile peppers
2 pounds flank steak, or your favorite cut
½ teaspoon salt
1 teaspoon black pepper, freshly ground
1 teaspoon garlic powder
2 cloves, freshly ground
2 tablespoons Cognac (optional)
3 tablespoons granulated sugar
1 drop red food coloring (optional)
2 tablespoons vegetable oil
⅓ cup Fish Sauce (*Nước Mắm Chấm*; see Chapter 6), plus more for garnish
1 cup soy sauce
3 tablespoons granulated sugar
⅓ cup honey, warmed
2 teaspoons sesame seeds, lightly toasted
6 tablespoons Pickled Papaya (*Gỏi Đu Đủ*; see Chapter 6)
2 tablespoons Thai basil leaves, coarsely chopped
2 tablespoons Vietnamese mint leaves, coarsely chopped

1. **Preparing the chiles:** Stem the chiles. Using a paring knife, cut a 2"–3" slit in the peppers. Remove some of the seeds (to reduce heat), and finely chop. Place in a mortar and pestle and mash into a coarse paste.

2. **Preparing the meat:** Place the beef in the freezer for at least 1 hour. Thinly slice the meat (depending on your preference, ⅛"–¼"-thick), using a sharp chef's knife. Make sure to cut the meat *with* the grain. Season with salt and pepper. Mix well.

3. **Seasoning the meat:** In a large mixing bowl, combine the garlic powder, cloves, Cognac (if using), sugar, red food coloring (if using), chiles, 1 tablespoon of the oil, ⅓ cup fish sauce, and soy sauce. Stir well. Pat the meat dry with paper towels, and then add the meat to the bowl. Mix until evenly coated. Seal and chill in the refrigerator for at least 4 hours, preferably overnight (up to 2 days).

4. **Drying the meat:** If you own a dehydrator, grease the trays with a little vegetable oil and arrange the beef, spreading the pieces so they're flat without covering each other. Follow the instructions for the machine (7 hours at 150°F is typical). If you don't have a dehydrator, arrange the meat on 2 oiled racks placed on top of 2 cookie sheets (to collect the excess liquid). It's fine if the slices touch each other, as they will shrink while drying. Preheat the oven to 250°F. Bake meat for 20 minutes, then turn the slices with tongs and lower the temperature to 200°F. Bake for 20–30 minutes more, until the beef looks dried out but remains malleable. To guarantee the perfect texture without too much moisture, leave the oven open slightly while baking; simply use a silicone oven mitt or any heatproof object to hold the door open.

5. **Sweetening the beef jerky:** In a small bowl, combine the warm honey with 2 teaspoons of the vegetable oil. Stir well. Brush a thin layer of honey onto the slices and sprinkle with lightly toasted sesame seeds. Return to the oven at 180°F for 40–45 minutes (with the oven slightly open, as in the previous step). The jerky should be slightly sticky but not hard. You can store the beef jerky in airtight containers for up to 2 months, or for several months in sealable bags in the refrigerator.

6. **Assembly time:** If the beef jerky is cold, reheat the beef slices on a greased grill, flipping the beef with chopsticks until both sides are slightly toasted and warm. Let it cool for about 30 seconds, then snip it into thin strips using kitchen shears. Add the pickled papaya (*gỏi đu đủ*) with as little moisture as possible (pat dry). Toss thoroughly. Set aside for about 10 minutes. Drain and discard the liquid; otherwise the mixture will be too watery and the sandwich will turn soggy. When you're ready to serve, add the chopped Thai basil and Vietnamese mint. Toss well.

7. **Sandwich assembly:** Use 1 baguette per serving. Cut lengthwise into the baguette and remove some of the crumb. Spread a thin layer of softened butter on one side and Lime Mayonnaise (*Sốt Ma Dô Ne*; see Chapter 6) on the other. Fill with the beef jerky/papaya mixture. Drizzle with *nước mắm chấm*. Add thinly sliced jalapeño pepper and the condiment(s) of your choice, such as Pickled Garlic (*Tỏi Chua Ngọt*; see Chapter 6). Garnish with 2 sprigs of cilantro. Close the sandwich tightly.

BEEF JERKY AND PAPAYA SALAD: *Gỏi Đu Đủ Khô Bò*

VIETNAMESE MEATBALLS

Xíu Mại Sốt Cà

YIELDS 8 SERVINGS

Like many Asian dishes, these meatballs were heavily inspired by their Occidental equivalent. The primary difference is that they're steamed in the sauce, not fried. The meatballs are filled with Asian ingredients such as shallots, leeks, water chestnuts, and *nước mắm* (fish sauce), then smothered in tomato sauce (*cà chua*).

¼ cup vegetable oil (or any neutral oil)

1 shallot, thinly sliced

2 pounds pork, freshly ground (or the meat of your choice)

¼ teaspoon baking powder

2½ tablespoons tapioca starch

½ white onion, finely chopped

3 tablespoons Chinese brown sugar (*đường thẻ*) (or regular brown sugar), to taste

1 tablespoon oyster sauce

1 teaspoon garlic powder

¼ teaspoon red chile powder

1 cup cooked water chestnuts (see sidebar), finely diced

2 tablespoons cooking wine (*rượu nấu ăn*) (optional)

1½ teaspoons salt, plus more to taste

1 teaspoon black pepper, coarsely ground, plus more to taste

1 (14-ounce) can chicken broth

2 cloves garlic, finely minced

1 (6") piece leek (white part only), washed and chopped

3 ripe tomatoes, chopped

2 tablespoons tomato paste

1 tablespoon Fish Sauce (*Nước Mắm Chấm*; see Chapter 6)

1. **Preparing the shallot:** Heat 2 teaspoons of the oil in a pan over medium-high heat and fry the shallot for 4 minutes until golden brown.

2. **Preparing the meat:** In a large bowl, combine the ground pork, baking powder, 1½ teaspoons of the tapioca starch, fried shallots, onion, brown sugar, oyster sauce, garlic powder, red chile powder, water chestnuts, and wine (if using). Season with salt and pepper. Mix well, cover with plastic wrap, and refrigerate for at least 2 hours.

3. **Key to proper seasoning:** In a small pan, heat about 1 teaspoon of the oil over high heat. Add about 1 tablespoon of the meat mixture. Cook for about 3 minutes. Taste and season with more salt and pepper if necessary.

4. **Forming the meatballs:** Grease your hands with oil and form about 40 golf-ball-sized meatballs.

5. **For the thickening agent:** In a small bowl, combine the remaining tapioca starch, ⅓ cup of the chicken broth, and the rest of the brown sugar. Stir well.

6. **Making the tomato sauce:** Heat the remaining oil in a large pot. Add the garlic and fry until golden. Add the meatballs and sear for 2–3 minutes until a thin outer crust is formed. Transfer to a plate (they will finish steaming in the tomato sauce). Add the leeks, and cook over low heat for about 10 minutes, stirring frequently to prevent them from burning, until the color is evenly golden brown. Add the tomatoes. Cook over high heat for about 30 minutes, stirring occasionally. Transfer to a food mill. If you don't have a food mill, you can use a food processor, then pass the sauce through a coarse-mesh sieve and discard the tomato skin, which can create an unpleasant texture. Return the tomato sauce to the pot, add the remaining chicken broth and tomato paste, and let simmer for 15 minutes. Season with salt and pepper; bring to a boil. Stir the tapioca starch mixture one more time and then add it to the tomato sauce, stirring constantly until slightly thickened. Return the meatballs to the pan. Cover and cook for 15 minutes. Stir in the fish sauce and sprinkle with black pepper.

7. **Sandwich assembly:** Use 1 baguette per serving. Cut lengthwise into the baguette and remove some of the crumb. Spread a thin layer of softened butter on one side and a thin layer of tomato sauce on the other. Arrange the meatballs on the bread. Drizzle with *nước mắm chấm* or Maggi Seasoning. Fill the sandwich with thin slices of jalapeño and the condiment(s) of your choice, such as Pickled Carrots and Daikon (*Đồ Chua;* see Chapter 6). Garnish with 2 sprigs of cilantro. Close the sandwich tightly. Serve with a bowl of tomato sauce on the side for dipping.

WATER CHESTNUTS   You can find fresh water chestnuts in most Asian markets. If you can't buy the fresh version, you can use canned water chestnuts or jicama (but both are slightly less crunchy). How to cook fresh water chestnuts: Wash the chestnuts in cold water, and then soak in lukewarm water for about 30 minutes. Soaking them softens the shell. With a paring knife, make a small crisscross cut at the root (bottom) of each water chestnut. Make sure that you don't cut into the flesh of the chestnut. Place the chestnuts in a pot and cover them with water. Bring to a gentle boil and cook for 30 minutes. Allow the chestnuts to cool just until you can easily handle them, and then shell and dice them.

VIETNAMESE MEATBALLS: *Xíu Mại Sốt Cà*

SHREDDED PORK COTTON

Chà Bông

YIELDS 12 SERVINGS

Bông means "cotton" in Vietnamese. It's meat "wool," also known as meat "floss." The meat is stewed and hand-shredded to give it a "dried" look, then further shredded into a fluffy texture comparable to cotton.

3 pounds pork shoulder (or any boneless meat of your choice)

1 tablespoon white pepper, freshly ground

1 teaspoon ground ginger

1 white onion

2 tablespoons vegetable oil, plus more as needed

½ cup soy sauce

2 cups water

1¼ cups granulated sugar

1½ teaspoons mushroom seasoning salt (*bột nêm*) (or regular salt)

¼ teaspoon red chile powder

2 teaspoons grated coconut (optional)

⅛ teaspoon turmeric powder

1. **Preparing the meat:** Slice the piece of meat horizontally into about 4"-thick slices (3 pieces). In a small bowl, combine 2 teaspoons of the white pepper with the ground ginger. Gently dry the pieces of meat using paper towels. Rub the meat with the dry rub. Set aside and let marinate for 15 minutes.

2. **Frying the onion:** Peel and slice the onion. Heat 2 tablespoons vetetable oil in a large nonstick pan. Working in batches and adding more oil as needed (for extra crispness), add the onions and fry for 6 minutes until crisp and golden brown. Transfer to a platter lined with paper towels to drain the oil.

3. **For the seasoning:** In a small bowl, combine the soy sauce and the remaining teaspoon of white pepper. Stir well.

4. **Boiling the meat:** Pour 2 cups of water into a small pot. Add the fried onions. Bring to a boil. Add the pieces of meat. Bring back to a boil, then lower the heat to medium-high. Season with 1 teaspoon mushroom seasoning salt and cook for about 45–50 minutes. Add the seasoning mixture. Stir well and cook until all the liquid is almost gone.

5. **Shredding the meat:** Remove the meat to a cutting board. Reserve the liquid that remains in the pot. Let the meat cool to room temperature. Using your fingers, shred the meat. In a wok, heat 1 teaspoon of the oil. Add ¼ cup of the sugar, the red chile powder, coconut, turmeric, and the remaining liquid from the pot. Stir well. Once it's boiling, add the shredded meat. Stir-fry until the meat is nearly dry. Season with ½ teaspoon mushroom seasoning salt.

6. **Making meat wool:** Add the remaining sugar to the wok, stirring constantly until the meat is dry-looking.

7. **Sandwich assembly:** Use 1 baguette per serving. Cut lengthwise into the baguette and remove some of the crumb. Drizzle the inside of the baguette with Fish Sauce (*Nước Mắm Chấm*; see Chapter 6) or Maggi Seasoning. Spread a thin layer of softened butter on one side of the bread. Fill the sandwich with the *chà bông* (shredded meat), sliced cucumbers, and Pickled Mango (*Gỏi Xoài Xanh*; see Chapter 6). Garnish with 2 sprigs of cilantro. Close the sandwich tightly.

HONEY-GLAZED BEEF

Bò Nướng Mật Ong

YIELDS 6 SERVINGS

Caramelized beef is a delicious meat choice for Vietnamese sandwiches. Beef is threaded onto skewers, then brushed with honey. All you need to add is a mixture of lime juice, salt, and pepper (the typical dipping sauce that goes with almost every Vietnamese meal).

2 pound boneless beef sirloin
½ teaspoon black pepper
¼ teaspoon baking powder
¼ teaspoon red chile powder
¼ cup honey
2 cloves garlic, finely minced
Juice of 1 lime
2 tablespoons soy sauce
4 tablespoons canola oil
1 tablespoon Fish Sauce (*Nước Mắm Chấm*; see Chapter 6)
1 green bell pepper
½ fresh pineapple, peeled and cubed
1 white onion, cut into wedges
1 tablespoon lightly toasted sesame seeds
½ teaspoon mushroom seasoning salt (*bột nêm*) (or regular salt)

1. **Preparing the meat:** Cut the beef diagonally across the grain into ¼"-thick slices. Sprinkle with black pepper, baking powder, and red chile powder. Mix well. Set aside.

2. **For the marinade:** In a bowl, combine 3 tablespoons of the honey, the garlic, lime juice, soy sauce, and 1 tablespoon of the oil. Place the meat in a mixing bowl. Add the marinade, mix well, and let sit for 30 minutes.

3. **Soaking the skewers:** While the meat is marinating, soak bamboo skewers in water. This step will prevent the bamboo from burning on the grill. You could also use nonstick metal skewers.

4. **Forming the beef skewers:** In a small bowl, combine the remaining 1 tablespoon honey and the fish sauce. Stir well and set aside. Thread the beef (discard the marinade) onto skewers, alternating with green pepper, pineapple, and onion. Drizzle with a little oil. Brush the grill of the barbecue (or indoor barbecue) with oil. Heat the grill to the highest setting and arrange the beef skewers on the hot grill. Cook for 3–4 minutes on each side for medium-rare meat (up to 5–6 minutes for medium). Remove skewers from the grill, brush with the honey/fish sauce mixture, sprinkle with sesame seeds, and transfer to a platter. Allow to rest for about 15 minutes. Sprinkle with a little mushroom seasoning salt (if necessary). Remove and discard the skewers.

5. **Sandwich assembly:** Use 1 baguette per serving. Cut lengthwise into the baguette and remove some of the crumb. Spread a layer of softened butter on one side and Lime Mayonnaise (*Sốt Ma Dô Ne*; see Chapter 6) on the other. Arrange the grilled beef, green pepper, pineapple, and onions, along with pieces of cucumber, Thai basil leaves, Vietnamese mint, and the condiment(s) of your choice, such as Pickled Papaya (*Gỏi Đu Đủ*) and Pickled Bean Sprouts (*Dưa Giá Với Hẹ Trái Táo Xanh*) (see Chapter 6 for both condiments). Garnish with 2 sprigs of cilantro. Close the sandwich tightly.

HEAD CHEESE

Giò Thủ

YIELDS 2 (8"-LONG) ROLLS

Head cheese is a cold lunchmeat originally from France that the North Vietnamese reproduced with an Asian twist. Meat from the head of a pig (or calf) is mixed with the animal's ears, star anise, garlic, peppercorns, pistachios, wood ear mushrooms, and fish sauce. Once cooked and cooled, the meat takes on a gelatinous texture. *Giò Thủ* adds a slight crunch and balance of texture in *bánh mì* sandwiches. It's usually prepared in anticipation of the *Tết*, the Vietnamese New Year celebration.

4 cheeks (pig or calf)

8 ears (pig or calf)

1 tongue

¼ cup salt

2 cups white vinegar

1 (4") chunk fresh ginger

1 yellow onion

2 star anise, crushed

¼ cup grated Chinese brown sugar (*đường thẻ*) (or regular brown sugar)

1 tablespoon salt

Undyed 100 percent cotton sheet fabric, for lining 2 (15-ounce) empty cans

2 tablespoons vegetable oil

4 garlic cloves, minced

3 shallots, finely chopped

¾ cup wood ear mushrooms

1 teaspoon mushroom seasoning salt (*bột nêm*) (or regular salt)

2 tablespoons Fish Sauce (*Nước Mắm Chấm*; see Chapter 6)

1 teaspoon white pepper

2 tablespoons whole black peppercorns

2 tablespoons pistachio kernels, blanched, skin removed

1. **Cleaning the meat:** Place the cheeks, ears, and tongue in a small pot. Add 2 tablespoons of the salt and the vinegar. Cover completely with cold water. Stir well and let sit for 15 minutes. Drain and rinse.

2. **Charring the ginger and yellow onion:** Wash the whole unpeeled ginger; pat dry. Peel the whole onion without cutting the stem to make sure the onion doesn't fall apart in the broth. Place a grill on your stove, heat to the highest setting, then char all the skin of the ginger and onion. Wrap them in aluminum foil. Let cool for about 10 minutes. Wash the ginger and onion under running tap water; the blackened skin will come right off. Bruise the ginger using a hammer to loosen the flesh and help release the flavor.

3. **Boiling the meat:** Place the charred ginger, onion, and star anise in a large pot. Add the ears, tongue, and cheeks; cover with water. Bring the liquid to a boil, then lower the heat to a bubbly simmer. Cook for 40 minutes until softened. Regularly skim the impurities rising to the surface of the broth using a fine mesh strainer. Add 2 tablespoons of the brown sugar and 1 tablespoon salt. Stir well and cook for another 5–10 minutes until a fork can easily poke through the ears without resistance. Using a slotted spoon, remove the meat from the water; transfer to a large bowl. Cover with cold water and set aside for about 15 minutes. (Note: This method, called "shocking," which ensures that the meat does not darken as the broth cools down, is the same procedure as that used to keep vegetables a bright green color.) At the end of that time, drain the water. Using a sharp chef's knife, thinly slice all the meat. Remove and discard the ginger, star anise, and onion.

4. **Preparing the cans:** Remove both ends of 2 empty (15-ounce) cans with a can opener. Set the removed ends aside; do not discard them. Line the inside of the cans with undyed 100 percent cotton sheet fabric.

5. **Cooking the meat:** Heat the oil in a large pan. Add the garlic. Cook for 2–3 minutes over medium-high heat until fragrant. Add the shallots and cook for 6–7 minutes until softened and golden brown. Add the thinly sliced meat. Sauté and cook for 8–9 minutes, stirring constantly. Add the wood ear mushrooms and cook for 2 minutes. Add the remaining sugar, mushroom seasoning salt, fish sauce, and white pepper. Toss well. Turn off the heat, then add the

whole black peppercorns and pistachios. Fill the cans with the hot mixture, making sure it's tightly packed (squeeze down the mixture to ensure that it's packed well). When the cans are filled, fold the cotton fabric at the ends, as if you were wrapping a gift. Seal the ends with the plastic wrap liners, and then top the plastic with the reserved metal ends of the cans. Wrap the cans in plastic wrap. Let cool to room temperature and then chill in the refrigerator for at least 4 hours.

6. **Sandwich assembly for a "special combo _bánh mì_":**
   Unmold the roll and cut into thin slices using a sharp knife (or a meat slicer). Use 1 baguette per serving. Cut lengthwise into the baguette and remove some of the crumb. Spread a layer of Pâté (_Ba Tê Gan Xay_; see Chapter 3) on one side and Lime Mayonnaise (_Sốt Ma Dô Ne_; see Chapter 6) on the other. Arrange thinly sliced Vietnamese-Style Cold Cuts (_Thịt Nguội_, in this chapter), and thinly sliced Head Cheese (_Giò Thủ_). Add sliced _chả lụa_ of your choice (see Vegetarian Bologna Sausage (_Chả Lụa Chay_), Chapter 2; Chicken Bologna Sausage (_Chả Lụa Gà Chiên_), Chapter 3; or Steamed Ham Roll (_Chả Lụa Bì_), Chapter 4), sliced jalapeño pepper, a few pieces of cucumber, and the condiment(s) of your choice, such as Pickled Carrots and Daikon (_Đồ Chua_; see Chapter 6). Garnish with 2 sprigs of cilantro. Close the sandwich tightly.

FERMENTED PORK ROLL

Nem Chua

YIELDS 6 SERVINGS

Nem Chua is a fermented pork roll. *Chua* translates to "sour." This method of preparation makes the most delicious lunchmeats that are generally served cold on sandwiches.

½ (1-pound) package frozen cooked sliced pork skin, thawed

1 teaspoon salt

1–1½ pounds ground pork (pork sirloin), or the meat of your choice, such as beef

4 cloves garlic, freshly grated

2 cloves garlic, cut into quarters

2 tablespoons whole black peppercorns

2 teaspoons black pepper, coarsely cracked

¼ cup palm sugar, freshly grated (or granulated sugar)

1 (2.4-ounce) package *nam* seasoning powder mix

8 fresh red Thai chiles, stemmed and cut into thirds

4 cloves garlic, very thinly sliced

1. **Preparing the pork skin:** Place the thawed pork skin in lukewarm salted water (cover the meat completely with warm water and add 1 teaspoon salt). Cover and let sit for 30 minutes. Stir every now and then so it doesn't form one block. Drain thoroughly and pat dry with paper towels, removing as much liquid as possible. Cut into thin strips, 2"–3" long.

2. **Preparing the meat:** In a large bowl, combine the ground pork, pork skin, grated garlic, garlic quarters, whole peppercorns, cracked pepper, sugar, *nam* seasoning powder mix, and chile pieces. Mix until evenly distributed. Form meat into 3" squares. Place a few garlic slices on an individual square of plastic wrap and top with a patty. Repeat for all of the meat. Tightly wrap the plastic around each patty, securing it with additional rubber bands if necessary to make sure there are no air bubbles. Place the wrapped patties in a baking pan, packing them closely together. When the pan is full, place another flat baking pan inside of it, with a heavy weight on top to press the patties down. Cover the entire pan with plastic wrap and refrigerate for at least 48 hours. The color of the meat will become pink. These patties can be stored for up to 1 week.

3. **Assembly time:** Purists eat *nem chua* as-is (raw) with *rau răm* leaves (Vietnamese coriander), but for food safety, unwrap them and place them on a hot grill and cook until you see charring marks.

4. **Sandwich assembly:** Use 1 baguette per serving. Cut lengthwise into the baguette and remove some of the crumb. Spread a layer of softened butter on one side. Arrange the *nem chua* patties on the baguette, and top with the condiment(s) of your choice, such as sliced lettuce, thinly sliced jalapeño, sliced cucumber, and Pickled Carrots and Daikon (*Đồ Chua*) (see Chapter 6). Garnish with 2 sprigs of cilantro. Close the sandwich tightly.

SHREDDED PORK

Bì

YIELDS 6 SERVINGS

Bì is cooked meat that is finely shredded, mixed with shredded pork skin, then tossed in dry-roasted rice powder. In general, it's served at room temperature in the *bánh mì* along with *xá xíu* (grilled pork) and a drizzle of *nước mắm chấm* (fish sauce).

½ cup jasmine rice

1 pound pork shoulder (or boneless meat of your choice)

1½ tablespoons garlic powder

¼ teaspoon baking powder

1 tablespoon mushroom seasoning salt (*bột nêm*) (or regular salt)

¼ cup vegetable oil (or any neutral oil), as needed

¼ cup green onions, chopped

3 garlic cloves, minced

1 (4") piece galangal (see sidebar), peeled and finely chopped

½ (1-pound) package frozen pre-cooked, sliced pork skin, thawed

1 tablespoon palm sugar, freshly grated (or granulated sugar)

¼ teaspoon red chile powder

1 teaspoon salt

1 teaspoon black pepper, freshly ground

1 large yellow onion, thinly sliced

1. **For the dry-roasted rice powder:** Dry-roast the jasmine rice in a medium sauté pan on the stove. Stir the rice using chopsticks until the grains turn a rich brown color (about 5–7 minutes over high heat). Let cool. Grind the grains into a fine powder using a food processor or spice grinder.

2. **Preparing the meat:** Slice the meat horizontally into about 2½"-thick slices (4 slices). In a small bowl, combine garlic powder, baking powder, and 2 teaspoons of the mushroom seasoning salt. Gently pat the meat dry using paper towels. Rub the meat with the dry rub. Set aside and let marinate for 15 minutes.

3. **Cooking the meat:** In a large pan, heat the oil. Add the green onions. Cook until softened and fragrant. Transfer to a bowl, leaving about 2–3 tablespoons of oil in the pan. In the same pan, add the garlic and fry until golden. Add the galangal and cook for 1 minute until fragrant but not browned. Transfer to another bowl, leaving all the oil in the pan. In the same pan, reheat the oil (you can add more if necessary), and add the pieces of meat. Sear the meat on both sides. Once an outer crust is formed, cover the meat and lower the heat to the lowest setting. Cook for about 10 minutes, flipping the pieces of meat periodically until the liquid released during cooking evaporates. Once the meat is cooked, transfer to a plate. Cover with a piece of aluminum foil and let cool to room temperature. Cut into thin slices, then cut into thin shreds 2"–3" long.

4. **Preparing the pork skin:** Place the thawed pork skin in lukewarm salted water. Cover and let sit for 30 minutes. Stir every now and then so it doesn't form one block. Drain thoroughly and pat dry with paper towels, removing as much liquid as possible. Cut the slices into thin shreds 2"–3"-long.

5. **Making bì:** In a mixing bowl, combine the shredded meat, shredded skin, remaining mushroom seasoning salt, sugar, and red chile powder. Toss well. Add about 4 tablespoons rice powder. Toss the meat salad in the rice powder until well combined. Add the reserved fried garlic and galangal. Taste and adjust seasoning with salt and black pepper. Toss well, then sprinkle with more (about 1 tablespoon) rice powder. Mix well.

6. **Frying the onions:** In the same pan, heat the oil over high heat. Once the oil is hot, add the onions and fry for 6–8 minutes until golden brown, stirring occasionally to prevent them from burning. Set aside.

7. **Sandwich assembly:** Use 1 baguette per serving. Cut lengthwise into the baguette and remove some of the crumb. Drizzle the inside of the baguette with *nước mắm chấm* or Maggi Seasoning. Spread a thin layer of softened butter on one side of the bread. Fill the sandwich with *bì*, *Char Siu* Barbecue Pork (*Thịt Xá Xíu*; see recipe in this chapter), sliced cucumbers, fried onions, and Pickled Mango (*Gỏi Xoài Xanh*; see Chapter 6). Garnish with 2 sprigs of cilantro. Close the sandwich tightly.

GALANGAL Galangal belongs to the same family as ginger but the color is less intense. You can find the rhizome (the underground stem of a plant, which sends off roots) of this plant in most Asian markets. If not, you can substitute double the amount of ginger for the galangal, as ginger is less aromatic and not as strong in flavor.

CHAPTER 5

SEAFOOD SANDWICHES

Vietnam, as the easternmost country on the Indochina Peninsula in Southeast Asia, is blessed with a plethora of seafood dishes. With choices such as Crab Cakes (*Nem Cua Biển*) and Seafood Meatloaf (*Mắm Lóc Chưng Thịt*), you'll be able to prepare a feast of *bánh mì* that celebrates the fruits of the sea. For the adventurous, consider Dill Fish (*Chả Cá Thăng Long*) or Ginger Sardine (*Cá Mòi Kho Gừng*). Like all *bánh mì* dishes, the recipes are very adaptable and you can easily substitute a milder ingredient if you're not feeling particularly adventuresome.

The recipes in this chapter are for typical seafood *bánh mì* fillings, ones you would find in a *bánh mì* shop. In general, use 1 small authentic Vietnamese baguette per serving, or ⅓ of a larger French baguette. (Try making your own! See the Vietnamese Baguette: *Bánh Mì Baguette* recipe in Chapter 1.) For each recipe, the final step includes sandwich assembly instructions. You can choose to use the suggested ingredients, or mix and match your favorite flavors to taste. The listed ingredients are a general guide, and you can customize your sandwiches for a unique *bánh mì* experience every time.

GINGER SARDINE

Cá Mòi Kho Gừng

YIELDS 6 SERVINGS

Cá Mòi Kho Gừng is a flavorful sardine dish in ginger sauce. Sardines that are carelessly prepared can sometimes have a rather strong flavor, but pairing them with lots of shallots and ginger turns them into a wonderful filling for a Vietnamese sandwich. These sardines taste even better the day after they're made, so if possible, prepare them in advance.

1 (6") piece fresh ginger

1½ pounds small fresh sardines

2 tablespoons white vinegar

½ teaspoon red chile powder

3 tablespoons vegetable oil

6 shallots, finely chopped

2 cloves garlic, freshly grated

2 tablespoons sugar

2 tablespoons water

2 tablespoons Fish Sauce (*Nước Mắm Chấm*; see Chapter 6), plus more for drizzling

¾ teaspoon mushroom seasoning salt (*bột nêm*) (or regular salt)

1 teaspoon black pepper, freshly ground

2 tablespoons green onions, cut into 1" pieces

½ lime

1. **Preparing the ginger:** Clean the chunk of ginger and peel it with the edge of a spoon; grate 1½ tablespoons. Thinly slice the rest and cut the slices into ½"-long matchsticks. Set aside.

2. **Preparing the sardines:** Leave the skin on the sardines. Using kitchen shears, trim off the heads and discard them. Clean the inside of each fish thoroughly under running water. Place the sardines in a deep dish. Barely cover with water and add the vinegar. Mix well and let stand for about 5 minutes. Discard the water. Pat sardines dry using paper towels. Sprinkle the insides with red chile powder and grated ginger. Note: If the sardines are too large, the bones might not be edible. If so, carefully pick out all bones (pin and belly) using tweezers.

3. **Preparing the shallots:** Use a heavy-bottomed pan with its matching lid. Add 2 tablespoons of the vegetable oil. Once the oil is hot, add the shallots. Cook the shallots for about 6–8 minutes until soft and nicely golden. Leaving as much oil as possible in the pan, transfer the shallots to a platter. Set aside.

4. **Cooking the fish:** Pat the sardines dry one more time. Using a brush, lightly coat the sardines with the remaining oil; set aside. In the pan used for the shallots, cook the ginger matchsticks until golden. Add the garlic and cook until fragrant (1–2 minutes). Add the sardines to the pan, arranging them in one layer. Pan-sear for 1 minute; flip the fish and sear the other side for 1 minute. Transfer the fish to a platter. Set aside.

5. **Assembly time:** In the same pan, dissolve the sugar with 2 tablespoons water over high heat. It's important to carefully watch the sugar; as soon as the sugar at the edges of the pan starts caramelizing (changing color), immediately lower the heat to medium-low. Gently move the pan in circles. Don't let the sugar get dark brown or it will burn. When all the sugar is an amber color, remove the pan from the heat, let it sit for 1 minute, and then slowly add the fish sauce, stirring constantly with a wooden spoon to keep the liquid from splattering. Return the sardines and shallots to the pan. Season with mushroom seasoning salt and black pepper. Add just enough water to barely cover the fish. Bring to a boil, cover the pan, lower the heat, and then gently simmer for about 20 minutes, depending on the size

of the fish. Add green onions. Cover and let sit for 10 minutes. Check the doneness of the fish (add more water and cook a bit longer if not fully cooked); the tail should split and break very easily. Squeeze the lime and drizzle the juice over the fish.

6. **Sandwich assembly:** Use 1 baguette per serving. Cut lengthwise into the baguette and remove some of the crumb. Drizzle the inside of the baguette with *nước mắm chấm*. Spread a thin layer of softened butter on one side of the bread. Delicately divide the fish in half lengthwise and fill the sandwich with long pieces of sardines, cucumbers, and the condiment(s) of your choice, such as Pickled Mango (*Gỏi Xoài Xanh*; see Chapter 6). Garnish with crushed roasted peanuts and 2 sprigs of cilantro. Close the sandwich tightly.

GINGER SARDINE: *Cá Mòi Kho Gừng*

SEAFOOD MEATLOAF

Mắm Lóc Chưng Thịt

YIELDS 7 MINI FISH LOAVES

This "meatloaf" is a staple of Vietnamese cuisine. It's a blend of ground meat (pork or chicken), crabmeat, salted snakehead fish fillet in brine, bean thread noodles, mushrooms, and eggs. *Mắm Lóc Chưng Thịt* has a characteristically pungent flavor, so if you're looking for a real taste of Vietnam, you've found it.

1 uncooked Dungeness crab

1–1½ cups water

½ (2-ounce) package dried bean thread noodles

8 eggs

2 egg whites

1½ teaspoons mushroom seasoning salt (*bột nêm*) (or regular salt)

½ teaspoon yellow food coloring powder

1 (6-ounce) jar salted snakehead fish fillet in brine

1 pound ground pork

1½ teaspoons ginger garlic paste

1½ yellow onions, finely diced

½ teaspoon red chile powder

1½ teaspoons black pepper

3 tablespoons green onions, finely chopped

4 tablespoons cilantro, finely chopped, plus 7 whole leaves

1 teaspoon sugar

6 fresh wood ear mushrooms, finely chopped

1(15-ounce) can straw mushrooms, drained and halved

1 tablespoon canola oil

1. **Preparing the crab:** Clean the crab, brush the abdominal flaps and in between the claws, and rinse thoroughly. Place in a pot, add about 1–1½ cups of water, and bring to a boil for about 10–15 minutes (count approximately 8 minutes per pound). Transfer to an ice-water bath for about 3 minutes to stop the cooking process. Drain and discard all liquid. Remove and discard the abdominal flaps (the triangle-shaped tail). Lift and separate the back fin along with the rest of the claws: Place a spoon at the bottom of the crab, where the opening from the abdominal flaps are located, and use the stem of the spoon as a lever to lift the back fin. Remove and discard the "lungs" (also known as devil's fingers); they have a spongy texture and are inedible. Gently remove the crabmeat from the back fins (the inner chambers are filled with meat). Gently crack the claws using a meat tenderizer mallet, remove the meat from the claws, and place all the crabmeat in a large mixing bowl.

2. **Preparing the bean thread noodles:** Place the dried bean thread noodles in a bowl, cutting and discarding the little threads. Soak the noodles in cold water for 20 minutes and drain. Chop into 1" pieces. Set aside.

3. **Preparing the eggs:** Using a fork, combine 6 of the eggs, the 2 egg whites, and the mushroom seasoning salt. In another bowl, beat remaining 2 eggs with the yellow food coloring.

4. **Preparing the salted fish in brine:** Pat the fish fillet dry with paper towels. Remove and discard the bones. Thinly slice the fish. Pulse the fish into a fine moist powder using a mini-food processor. Set aside.

5. **Making the meatloaf mixture:** Reserve 7 cilantro leaves for decoration. Add the ground pork to the large mixing bowl containing the crabmeat. Season with ginger garlic paste, chopped onions, red chile powder, and black pepper. Using food service disposable gloves, mix all the ingredients in the bowl. Add the green onions, cilantro, sugar, and the mixture of 6 eggs and 2 egg whites. Add the wood ear mushrooms, the halved straw mushrooms, and bean thread noodles. Mix well.

6. **Key to proper seasoning:** In a small pan, heat about 1 teaspoon of the oil. Add about 1 tablespoon of the meatloaf mixture. Cook for 2–3 minutes. Taste and season with more salt and pepper if necessary.

7. **Steaming and baking:** Lightly spray some oil on 7 (6" diameter) disposable pot pie pans. Remove the excess oil. Fill each tin with meat mixture. Fill a large pot with cold water until it barely touches the steamer rack level. It's important to start with cold water so the fish loaves cook evenly. Place all the tins in the steamer (you may need to stack 2 levels to fit all the tins), bring to a boil, and reduce the heat to medium-high. Steam for about 15 minutes. Turn off the heat. Allow to rest for about 5 minutes. Preheat the oven to 350°F. Remove the tins from the steamer and transfer to a baking sheet. Evenly coat each tin with the 2 remaining eggs mixed with yellow food coloring. Garnish with a leaf of cilantro in the middle of each tin and bake for 15 minutes until the top is dried.

8. **Sandwich assembly:** Unmold the fish loaves and cut into long, thick slices. Use 1 baguette per serving. Cut length-wise into the baguette and remove some of the crumb. Spread a thin layer of softened butter on one side. Place the *mắm lóc chưng thịt* slices in the sandwich. Drizzle the inside of the baguette with Fish Sauce (*Nước Mắm Chấm;* see Chapter 6). Add cucumbers and the condiment(s) of your choice, such as Pickled Bean Sprouts (*Dưa Giá Với Hẹ Trái Táo Xanh*) and Pickled Carrots and Daikon (*Đồ Chua*) (see Chapter 6 for both condiments). Garnish with 2 sprigs of cilantro. Close the sandwich tightly.

GINGER GARLIC PASTE Ginger and garlic are very common ingredients in Vietnamese cooking. They're blended in advance into a paste for faster prep time: Simply clean a piece of fresh ginger, carefully removing any dirt. Peel the ginger root with a paring knife or the edge of a spoon, then grate it using a microplane. Place the grated ginger and garlic in a mortar and pestle and add about 1 tablespoon (or more) water for easy grinding. Turn the mixture into a thick paste. Store for up to 2 weeks in the refrigerator.

FRIED CATFISH

Cá Chiên

YIELDS 6 SERVINGS

Cá chiên can be made with any fish but the one most commonly used is catfish. The preparation is simple but like many simple things, each detail really counts. Follow this recipe step by step and you'll have delicious, crispy fish sticks to fill your *bánh mì*.

2 pounds catfish fillets
2 teaspoons onion powder
3 cloves garlic, crushed and finely minced
1 tablespoon cooking wine
1 teaspoon ground ginger
½ teaspoon red chile powder
½ cup canola oil, as needed
2 teaspoons salt, as needed to taste
⅓ cup all-purpose flour, as needed

1. **Marinating the fish:** Wash the fish and pat dry using paper towels. Cut the fillets into 1½"-thick rectangular sticks. Place in a shallow dish. Season the fish with onion powder, 2 teaspoons of the garlic, cooking wine, ginger, and red chile powder. Toss well. Drizzle with 1 tablespoon of the oil. Marinate the fish for no more than 30 minutes.

2. **Coating the fish sticks:** Pat the fish dry one more time and remove any moisture. Season with salt. Transfer a few fish sticks at a time onto a plate. Using a fine mesh strainer, sprinkle some flour over the fish sticks; shake off the excess flour.

3. **Dredging the fish:** Right before placing the fish on the skillet, gently shake the excess flour off each fish stick one more time. Dredging the fish in flour keeps the moisture in and makes a golden outer crust. Once you add the flour, fry the fish fillets right away. If you wait too long, the moisture from the fish will make them soggy.

4. **Frying the fish:** In a skillet, heat the remaining oil and fry the remaining garlic over medium-high heat until golden. Remove the garlic and set aside. Place the fish in the hot oil, making sure the fish sticks don't touch each other. Jiggle the pan to make sure the fish doesn't stick to the bottom of the pan and that the fish is totally coated with oil. Cook for 2–3 minutes until the first side is lightly golden. Using wooden chopsticks or a slotted fish turner, flip each piece and pan-fry the other side for another 2–3 minutes until crispy and lightly browned. To check the "doneness," cut a fish stick in half; the inside should be white and opaque. If it's still clear to translucent, cook the fish sticks a few minutes more. When the fish is fully cooked, jiggle the pan again. Remove the fish sticks to a plate covered with a paper towel. Repeat until all the sticks are used.

5. **Sandwich assembly:** Use 1 baguette per serving. Cut lengthwise into the baguette and remove some of the crumb. Spread a thin layer of butter on one side and Lime Mayonnaise (*Sốt Ma Dô Ne*; see Chapter 6) on the other side of the bread. Carefully fill the sandwich with the fish sticks, placed lengthwise. Drizzle the inside of the baguette with Fish Sauce (*Nước Mắm Chấm*; see Chapter 6). Add sliced cucumbers and the condiment(s) of your choice, such as Pickled Asparagus (*Gỏi Măng Tây*) or Beet Pickles (*Củ Cải Đường Muối Chua*) (see Chapter 6 for both condiments). Garnish with 2 sprigs of cilantro. Close the sandwich tightly.

VIETNAMESE-STYLE GRILLED SQUID

Mực Nướng Xả Ớt

YIELDS 6 SERVINGS

Mực Nướng Xả Ớt are grilled lemongrass-stuffed baby squid. The squid skewers are quickly grilled, then seasoned in a spicy dressing. The highlight of this healthy seafood dish is the addition of Vietnamese pea shoot tendrils, called *rau muống*.

2 tablespoons cilantro

2 tablespoons Vietnamese mint

2 cloves Pickled Garlic (*Tỏi Chua Ngọt*; see Chapter 6)

2 tablespoons chile garlic sauce

Juice of 1 lime

1 tablespoon palm sugar, grated

2 tablespoons soy sauce

1 bunch fresh lemongrass stalks

3 pounds frozen baby squid, pre-cleaned (tentacles removed)

1 (1") piece fresh ginger, thinly sliced

1½ pounds Vietnamese pea shoot tendrils (*rau muống*)

3 tablespoons vegetable oil, plus extra for drizzling

2 teaspoons freshly grated ginger

⅛ teaspoon turmeric (powder)

½ teaspoon salt

¼ teaspoon black pepper, coarsely ground

1 tablespoon Fish Sauce (*Nước Mắm Chấm*; see Chapter 6)

1 yellow onion, cut into thin wedges

1. **Preparing the skewers:** Soak bamboo skewers in water for at least 30 minutes. This step will prevent the bamboo from burning on the grill. You could also use nonstick metal skewers.

2. **Making the marinade:** Using a mortar and pestle, combine the cilantro, mint, pickled garlic, chile garlic sauce, 1 teaspoon lime juice, sugar, and soy sauce. Grind into a coarse paste.

3. **Preparing the lemongrass:** Wash the lemongrass, removing the white powder from the leaves. Cut the stalks into 2½" pieces. Crush the stalks with the back of a chef's knife and set aside.

4. **Preparing the squid:** In a large mixing bowl, combine the squid, lemongrass pieces, and ginger slices. Add ¾ of the marinade, reserving the rest for basting later. Toss until well coated. Let the flavors infuse for 10 minutes. In the meantime, prepare the pea shoot tendrils.

5. **Preparing the pea shoot tendrils:** Wash the pea shoots thoroughly in several baths. The greens tend to be sandy, so wash them carefully. Remove and discard any older, fibrous parts of the stems. Drain as much water as possible. Cut the stems into 5" sections.

6. **Stir-frying the pea shoot tendrils:** In a wok, heat the oil over high heat, almost to smoking point (this is very important; the high heat keeps the greens from releasing their liquid). Add the grated ginger and cook until it's aromatic. Add the pea shoots. Toss the vegetables for 3–4 minutes. The pea shoots are going to wilt and become shiny. Add turmeric, salt, and pepper. Transfer the pea shoots to a platter.

7. **Grilling time:** Add the fish sauce to the reserved marinade, stir well, and set aside. Stuff a piece of lemongrass and a ginger slice inside each squid. Thread the head of the squid onto a skewer, along with an onion wedge. Drizzle with a little oil. Brush the grill of the barbecue (outdoor or indoor) with oil. Heat the barbecue and arrange the squid skewers on the hot grill. Cook for 1–2 minutes on each side, basting the squid with reserved marinade. Squid cooks very quickly; don't overcook or it will become unpleasantly tough and chewy. Remove the skewers from the grill, brush with more reserved marinade, and place the skewers on a platter. Drizzle with lime juice. Check seasoning and sprinkle with a

little salt (if necessary). Remove the skewers; discard them if they're bamboo. Discard the lemongrass and ginger slices. Add the squid to the platter with the greens, and set the grilled onions aside.

8. **Sandwich assembly:** Use 1 baguette per serving. Cut lengthwise into the baguette and remove some of the crumb. Spread a layer of butter on one side and Lime Mayonnaise (*Sốt Ma Dô Ne*; see Chapter 6) on the other. Arrange the grilled squid, grilled onions, and *rau muống* (with as little liquid as possible). Drizzle the inside of the baguette with *nước mắm chấm* and add the condiment(s) of your choice, such as Pickled Papaya (*Gỏi Đu Đủ*) and Pickled Garlic (*Tỏi Chua Ngọt*) (see Chapter 6 for both condiments). Garnish with 2 sprigs of cilantro. Close the sandwich tightly.

VIETNAMESE-STYLE GRILLED SQUID:
Mực Nướng Xả Ớt

MANGO GRILLED SHRIMP

Tôm Nướng Cay Hương Vị Xoài

YIELDS 6 SERVINGS

This smoked shrimp dish has an intense flavor combination: a sweet fruit marinade with lingering heat. Your guests will ask for more! Once grilled, the texture of the shrimp is crisp, firm, and slightly crunchy. Here's another excuse to make good use of your barbecue grill during the summer!

2 tablespoons chile garlic sauce, store-bought

1 teaspoon garlic powder

1 (2") piece freshly grated ginger

¼ cup canned Kesar mango pulp (or any sweet fruit purée)

2 tablespoons grated Chinese brown sugar (*đường thẻ*) (or regular brown sugar)

1 tablespoon soy sauce

2 pounds frozen jumbo shrimp, thawed

2 teaspoons tapioca starch

½ teaspoon black pepper, coarsely ground

1 tablespoon Fish Sauce (*Nước Mắm Chấm*; see Chapter 6)

2 tablespoons vegetable oil

Juice of 1 lime

¼ teaspoon salt

1. **Preparing the skewers:** Soak bamboo skewers in water for at least 30 minutes. This step will prevent the bamboo from burning on the grill. You could also use nonstick metal skewers.

2. **Making the marinade:** In a small bowl, combine the chile garlic sauce, garlic powder, ginger, mango pulp, brown sugar, and soy sauce. Stir well.

3. **Preparing the shrimp:** If necessary, remove and discard the shrimp heads. Rinse the shrimp under cold running water and pat dry using paper towels. Sprinkle the shrimp with tapioca starch and black pepper. Transfer the shrimp to a sealable container and add ¾ of the marinade, reserving the rest for basting later. Seal and shake well. Make sure the marinade coats and penetrates the shrimp. Chill in the refrigerator for at least 1 hour.

4. **Assembly time:** Remove the shrimp from the refrigerator 15 minutes before cooking to bring them back to room temperature. Add fish sauce to the reserved marinade, stir well, and set aside. Thread the shrimp onto skewers. Drizzle with a little of the oil. Brush the grill of the barbecue (or indoor barbecue) with oil. Heat the grill and arrange the shrimp skewers on the hot grill. Cook for 3–4 minutes on each side, basting the shrimp with reserved marinade, until the shrimp change color and become opaque. Remove from the grill, brush with more marinade, and transfer to a platter. Allow to rest for about 10 minutes. Remove and discard the skewers. Shell the shrimp, and baste them with more reserved marinades. Drizzle with lime juice and sprinkle with a little salt (if necessary). The shrimp should have a dry crust on the outside and still be very moist on the inside. Remove and discard the skewers.

5. **Sandwich assembly:** Use 1 baguette per serving. Cut lengthwise into the baguette and remove some of the crumb. Spread a thin layer of butter on one side and Lime Mayonnaise (*Sốt Ma Dô Ne*; see Chapter 6) on the other. Arrange the grilled shrimp, pieces of cucumber, Thai basil leaves, Vietnamese mint, and the condiment(s) of your choice, such as Pickled Papaya (*Gỏi Đu Đủ*) and Pickled Bean Sprouts (*Dưa Giá Với Hẹ Trái Táo Xanh*) (see Chapter 6 for both condiments). Garnish with 2 sprigs of cilantro. Close the sandwich tightly.

MANGO   This dish can be made with a variety of flavors by using other canned tropical fruit purées, such as mangosteen, rambutan, star apple, pineapple, custard apple, longan, lychee, papaya, Hachiya persimmon, or dragonfruit. Be creative!

MANGO GRILLED SHRIMP:
Tôm Nướng Cay Hương Vị Xoài

VIETNAMESE GINGER SHRIMP STIR-FRY

Tôm Xào Gừng

YIELDS 6 SERVINGS

Tôm Xào Gừng has touches of sweet and spicy in the form of ginger, lychee, and chile. Cooking shrimp is always a delicate task; you have to make sure they're not overcooked, or they could become very chewy. Pay close attention to the cooking times recommended in this recipe.

1 (5") piece fresh ginger

1¼ pounds raw large shrimp

2 tablespoons palm sugar, freshly grated

1 cup water

4 cloves garlic, finely minced

½ cup salt

2 tablespoons red chile powder

1½ cups lychee liqueur (or cooking wine)

3 tablespoons canola oil

1 shallot, thinly sliced

1 chopped green onion

½ teaspoon salt

1½ tablespoons lychee jam (or your favorite preserves)

1 lime, freshly squeezed

½ teaspoon black pepper, freshly ground

1. **For the ginger:** Clean the ginger and peel it with a paring knife (or the edge of a spoon). Grate about 1" of ginger and cut the rest into slices lengthwise, then julienne the slices into matchstick-like pieces.

2. **Preparing the shrimp:** If necessary, remove and discard the shrimp heads. Carefully shell each shrimp, making sure not to remove the tail; this part is very delicate. Remove the black vein of each shrimp using a sharp, hook-like paring knife, all the way from the head to the tail, so when the shrimp are cooked, they will open up like butterflies. Rinse the shrimp under cold running water and pat dry using paper towels.

3. **Marinating the shrimp:** In a large bowl, dissolve the palm sugar in 1 cup water. Add the shrimp, half of the garlic, 1 tablespoon julienned ginger, salt, red chile powder, and 1 cup lychee liqueur. Let stand for about 30 minutes in the refrigerator. Drain the shrimp and pat dry using paper towels. There should be as little liquid as possible remaining on the shrimp.

4. **Cooking the shallots and green onions:** In a wok, heat the oil for 1–2 minutes over high heat. Add the shallots and fry for 4–5 minutes until golden brown. Add the green onions, stir-fry for 1 minute, and transfer to a plate, leaving as much oil as possible in the wok.

5. **Cooking ginger shrimp:** Warm the remaining lychee liqueur a few seconds in the microwave. Reheat the oil in the wok and then add the rest of the garlic and remaining julienned ginger. Cook until fragrant. Season the shrimp with ½ teaspoon salt. Carefully place the shrimp in the wok one piece at a time to avoid splattering. Cook for 1–2 minutes until seared on one side, then stir-fry the shrimp for 1 minute (if the wok is not large enough, you could stir-fry the shrimp in batches and keep warm under aluminum foil). The shrimp will begin to open and change color. Add the warm lychee liqueur. Immediately ignite the liqueur and allow to cook until all the flames disappear. It's not as scary as it seems but as a precaution, when flaming alcohol, have a fire extinguisher within reach. Add lychee jam (or your favorite preserves) and drizzle with lime juice. Stir well. Sprinkle with black pepper. Turn off the heat; top the shrimp with fried shallots and green onions.

6. **Sandwich assembly:** Use 1 baguette per serving. Cut lengthwise into the baguette and remove some of the crumb. Spread a thin layer of butter on one side of the bread and Lime Mayonnaise (*Sốt Ma Dô Ne*; see Chapter 6) on the other. Arrange the shrimp, sliced jalapeño pepper, lettuce, and the condiment(s) of your choice, such as Pickled Mango (*Gỏi Xoài Xanh*; see Chapter 6). Garnish with 2 sprigs of cilantro. Close the sandwich tightly.

DILL FISH

Chả Cá Thăng Long

YIELDS 6 SERVINGS

The attractive yellow color in this seafood dish from northern Vietnam comes from turmeric, which also adds fragrance. Dill (called *thì là* in Vietnamese) provides further aroma, while black sesame rice crackers (*bánh đa mè đen*) add a nice contrast in texture.

- 1 (1") chunk fresh galangal (or ginger)
- 2 pounds catfish fillets
- ¼ cup plain yogurt
- 2 teaspoons onion powder
- 3 cloves fresh garlic, crushed and finely minced
- ¾ teaspoon turmeric powder
- 3 tablespoons diced shallots
- 1 teaspoon grated palm sugar
- ½ teaspoon red chile powder
- ½ cup vegetable oil, as needed
- 2 teaspoons salt, or to taste
- ⅓ cup cornstarch, as needed
- 1 tablespoon all-purpose flour (optional)
- ½ cup green onions, cut into 1" pieces
- 1 small onion, cut into thin wedges
- 1 bunch fresh dill, coarsely chopped
- 2 tablespoons pure fish sauce
- ¼ cup coarsely chopped peanuts, roasted
- 3 fresh green chiles (optional), sliced
- 2 limes, cut into wedges
- 2 cups Fish Sauce (*Nước Mắm Chấm*; see Chapter 6)
- 3 cups combined shredded cucumber and Vietnamese herbs called *rau thơm* (mint, cilantro, perilla leaves, lettuce)
- 1 cup Pickled Bean Sprouts (*Dưa Giá Với Hẹ Trái Táo Xanh*; see Chapter 6)
- 1½ cups black sesame rice crackers

1. **Preparing the galangal:** Clean the chunk of galangal and remove any dirt. Peel the galangal root with the edge of a spoon, slice it, and then cut into julienne strips. Set aside.

2. **Preparing the fish:** Wash the fish and pat dry using paper towels. Cut the fillets into 1½"-thick fish sticks. Place in a shallow dish. Cover with plain yogurt and season the fish with onion powder, 3 teaspoons garlic, turmeric powder, shallots, galangal, palm sugar, and red chile powder. Mix until well coated. Drizzle with 1 tablespoon of the oil. Marinate the fish for no more than 30 minutes. Pat the fish dry one more time to remove any excess moisture. Season with salt. Transfer a few fish sticks at a time onto a plate. Using a fine mesh strainer, sprinkle cornstarch and some flour (if using) over the fish sticks; shake off the excess.

3. **Cooking the fish:** In a skillet, heat 4–5 tablespoons oil and fry the remaining garlic over medium heat until golden. Remove the garlic and set aside. Gently shake the excess flour off each fish stick one more time. Increase the heat to the highest setting and place the fish in the oil, making sure the fish sticks don't touch each other. Jiggle the pan to make sure the fish does not stick to the bottom of the pan and that the fish is totally coated with oil. Cook for 2–3 minutes until the first side is lightly golden. Using wooden chopsticks or a slotted fish turner, flip each piece and pan-fry the other side for another 2–3 minutes until crispy and lightly browned. To check the "doneness," cut a fish stick in half; the inside should be white and opaque. If it's still clear to translucent, cook the fish sticks a few minutes more. When the fish is fully cooked, jiggle the pan again. Remove the fish sticks to a plate covered with a paper towel. Repeat until all the sticks are used. In the same skillet, sauté the green onions and onion wedges until golden. Add half of the fresh dill; stir and cook at medium-low heat for 1 minute, until fragrant. Return the fish and fried garlic to the skillet. Season with a drizzle of fish sauce and cover with the remaining dill. Turn off the heat and sprinkle with peanuts. Jiggle the pan to let the flavors blend. Adjust seasoning if necessary. Discard the dill.

4. **Sandwich assembly:** Use 1 baguette per serving. Cut lengthwise into the baguette and remove some of the crumb. Spread a thin layer of softened butter on one side. Arrange the cucumber and combined Vietnamese herbs. Top with the fish and onions, a few slices of green chile pepper (if desired), coarsely crushed peanuts, and a drizzle of Fish Sauce (*Nước Mắm Chấm*; see Chapter 6), or more traditionally, Hanoi shrimp paste dipping sauce (*mắm ruốc*, which is quite pungent). Garnish with black sesame rice crackers and close the sandwich tightly.

VIETNAMESE-STYLE FRIED MUSSELS

Bánh Sò Chiên Giòn

YIELDS 4 SERVINGS

While traveling in Vietnam, your best bet is to eat delicious varieties of fried food; you'll also see wonderful street food vendors selling seafood. These very simple mussel fritters are typical of their offerings. The fritters most often are dipped in *nước mắm chấm* and paired with the usual *bánh mì* condiments.

1½ pounds mussels

2 cups all-purpose flour

2½ teaspoons salt

1 teaspoon sugar

1 teaspoon garlic powder

1 teaspoon red chile powder

1 teaspoon black pepper, freshly ground

1 quart peanut oil (or regular vegetable oil), for deep frying, as needed

½ cup tapioca starch

½ teaspoon turmeric

1 tablespoon baking powder

3 cups seltzer water (see sidebar)

1½ cups (8 ounces) crushed ice

¼ cup freshly ground rice flour (*bột gạo*)

6 frozen square eggroll wrappers, thawed (optional)

2 red Thai chiles, stemmed and sliced

1 chopped green onion

2 cloves garlic, finely minced

1. **Preparing the mussels:** If necessary, scrub the mussels under tap water. Place the mussels in a large mixing bowl. Add ¼ cup of the all-purpose flour and 1 teaspoon salt and soak for 30 minutes to let them disgorge any sand. Drain and pull the "beards" from the mussels, if any, with your fingers. Remove and discard any mussels that have opened.

2. **Shelling the mussels:** Place the mussels into a large pot in a single layer. Add water to a level of about 1". Cover and bring to a boil. Reduce to medium-low and cook for 5 minutes until the mussels open up (if any don't open, discard them). Scoop out the mussels with a spoon. Cut the white muscle and tendon free from each shell, transferring them to a mixing bowl as you go. Let cool to room temperature. Add ¼ teaspoon salt, ¾ teaspoon of the sugar, ½ teaspoon of the red chile powder, and pepper. Add about 2 teaspoons peanut oil. Toss well. Cover the bowl with plastic wrap and let the mussels marinate for 5 minutes in the refrigerator.

3. **For the fritter flour:** Combine remaining all-purpose flour, tapioca starch, turmeric, baking powder, remaining ¼ teaspoon sugar, garlic powder, ½ teaspoon red chile powder, and 1 teaspoon salt. Sift all the dry ingredients into another bowl.

4. **For the fritter batter:** Divide the seltzer water into 2 measuring cups: one with 2⅓ cups and another with ⅓ cup. Reserve the remaining amount. Add 2⅓ cups of seltzer water and crushed ice to the fritter flour until incorporated. Do not overmix; it's okay if the batter is still lumpy. In another bowl, dissolve the rice flour into ⅓ cup seltzer water. Combine the two mixtures and stir to combine evenly. Again, do not overmix. Mixing the batter lightly ensures that the cooked fritters will be airy. The consistency of the fritter batter should be similar to pancake batter; if necessary, add the remaining seltzer water and season with ¼ teaspoon salt. Allow the batter to rest for about 1 hour.

5. **Folding the wrappers (if using):** Separate the wrappers one at a time. Using kitchen shears, cut the wrappers in half diagonally, forming triangles. Place on a flat surface. Fold up the side flaps so they overlap, and then fold up the bottom flap and roll the wrapper away from you, forming a loose cigar shape. Using your fingers, moisten the tip of the wrapper with warm water so that the wrapper sticks together.

6. **For the chiles, onions, and crispy wrappers:** In a large Dutch oven (or any regular deep-fryer), heat 2" of oil for about 2 minutes over high heat. Add the fresh red chiles and green onions. Cook for 2 minutes until fragrant and transfer to a plate. In the same Dutch oven, add the folded wrappers and deep-fry for 2–3 minutes until golden brown. Transfer wrappers to the cooling rack, draining the excess oil on paper towels.

7. **Assembly time:** Place a cooling rack lined with paper towels on a baking sheet (for easy cleanup of the drained oil). Check to be sure the oil in the Dutch oven or deep-fryer is at least 2" deep. Heat the oil for about 2 minutes over high heat. Do not begin cooking until the oil is slightly bubbly; a thermometer should register 350°F–375°F (do not allow the oil to overheat). Lower the heat to medium. Dip a mussel into the fritter batter to coat completely. Raise the mussel and allow the excess batter to drip back into the bowl. Carefully place the mussel in the hot oil. Repeat the process for several more mussels. Fry the fritters in batches, making sure the fritters don't touch each other. As the fritters cook, they will start to pop and increase in volume; if necessary, place a splatter screen over the top of the Dutch oven. Deep-fry for 2–3 minutes until the fritters turn golden. Flip each piece using a spider skimmer and cook for about 1 minute more, until golden on all sides. Remove the fritters one at a time, draining as much oil as possible, and transfer them to the cooling rack. Continue with the remaining mussels. When all are fried, assemble the sandwich immediately.

8. **Sandwich assembly:** Use 1 baguette per serving. Cut lengthwise into the baguette and remove some of the crumb. Spread a thin layer of butter on one side and Lime Mayonnaise (*Sốt Ma Dô Ne*; see Chapter 6) on the other. Arrange the mussel fritters, red chiles, onions, crispy wrappers, sliced jalapeño pepper, lettuce, Thai basil, and Vietnamese mint in the sandwich. Drizzle with Fish Sauce (*Nước Mắm Chấm;* see Chapter 6). Add the condiment(s) of your choice, such as thinly sliced Pickled Garlic (*Tỏi Chua Ngọt*), Pickled Bean Sprouts (*Dưa Giá Với Hẹ Trái Táo Xanh*), and Pickled Mango (*Gỏi Xoài* Xanh) (see Chapter 6 for condiments). Garnish with 2 sprigs of cilantro. Close the sandwich tightly.

LIQUID CHOICE FOR THE FRITTER BATTER You can substitute club soda for the seltzer water, but if you do so you might want to omit the amount of salt used in the recipe. Another option is to use beer.

SUGARCANE SHRIMP CAKE

Chả Tôm

YIELDS 8 SERVINGS

Chả Tôm is the ultimate Vietnamese comfort (sea) food. Shrimp cakes are first shaped around skewers made of sugarcane and then grilled until firm. If you're not able to find fresh sugarcane (available in little Vietnamese shops in California), you can either used canned sugarcane sticks or simply use carrots or lemongrass stalks!

¼ cup peanut oil (or any neutral oil)

1 shallot, finely chopped

6 cloves garlic, finely minced

1½ pounds raw medium shrimp, thawed

4 frozen squid, thawed and diced

1 teaspoon red chile powder

1 tablespoon tapioca starch

1 tablespoon Chinese brown sugar (*đường thẻ*) (or regular brown sugar)

1 teaspoon granulated sugar

2 tablespoons ground *thịt ba rọi* (similar to pancetta) (optional)

2 teaspoons Fish Sauce (*Nước Mắm Chấm*; see Chapter 6)

1 small kaffir lime leaf, very finely chopped (optional)

2 egg whites

1⅓ teaspoons salt

¾ teaspoon black pepper

2½ pounds fresh sugarcane sticks, cut into 5"-long pieces

¼ cup green onions, chopped

2 teaspoons honey

1. **Frying the shallots and garlic:** Heat the oil in a small pan. Fry the shallots in the oil, stirring frequently to prevent them from burning, until the color is light brown. Add the garlic and fry until slightly golden.

2. **Preparing the seafood:** Remove and discard the shrimp heads if necessary. Shell and devein the shrimp using a sharp, hook-like paring knife, then coarsely chop. Pat shrimp and squid dry. Place the chopped shrimp and squid in the bowl of a food processor. Add the red chile powder, tapioca starch, brown sugar, granulated sugar, fried garlic and shallots (reserve the fragrant oil), and ground *thịt ba rọi* (if using). Pulse until smooth. Transfer to a mixing bowl. Add the fish sauce, chopped kaffir lime leaf (if using), egg whites, salt, and black pepper. Stir until combined. Cover with plastic wrap and let stand for 15 minutes to let the mixture firm up.

3. **Key for proper seasoning:** In a small pan, heat 1 teaspoon of peanut oil. Add 1 tablespoon of the shrimp mixture. Cook for about 3 minutes. Taste the shrimp. Season with more sugar, salt, and pepper, if necessary.

4. **Forming the *chả tôm*:** Add 2 teaspoons of the oil reserved from the shallots and garlic to the seafood mixture. Divide mixture into 24 equal portions. Grease your hands with a bit of oil. Form 5"-long oval shapes, place a sugarcane stick on top of each one lengthwise, and form the patties around the sticks so they act as skewers. Brush the shrimp cakes with a thin layer of the reserved oil.

5. **Steaming the *chả tôm*:** Add water to the bottom of a steamer to a depth of at least 2". Place the rack in the steamer. Line the rack with parchment paper and brush the paper with a little bit of the reserved oil. Bring the water to a boil, then lower the heat to medium-high. Place the shrimp cakes in the steamer, cover, and steam for about 5 minutes. The shrimp cakes should be soft and tender but still firm. Remove from the steamer and transfer to a plate. Let cool a little.

6. **For garnish:** In a small pan, heat the remaining reserved oil. Once it's hot, add the green onions and turn off the heat. Stir the green onions for 1 minute until softened, fragrant, and shiny. Transfer to a small bowl and set aside. While the oil is still hot, add the honey. Stir well.

7. **Grilling the *chả tôm*:** Preheat the oven to 170°F. Brush a flat griddle with peanut oil. Heat the barbecue grill (or indoor grill). Arrange the shrimp cakes on the hot grill. Cook for 4–5 minutes on each side until golden. The *chả tôm* should have a dry crust on the outside and still be very moist on the inside. Brush the shrimp with a thin layer of the honey/oil mixture while still hot. Once the shrimp cakes are cooked, transfer them to the oven and keep them warm until you're ready to assemble the sandwiches.

8. **Sandwich assembly:** Use 1 baguette per serving. Cut lengthwise into the baguette and remove some of the crumb. Spread a thin layer of butter on one side and Lime Mayonnaise (*Sốt Ma Dô Ne*; see Chapter 6) on the other. Cut the *chả tôm* in half lengthwise. Add the halved pieces to the sandwich and cover with the reserved green onions. Drizzle the inside of the baguette with Fish Sauce (*Nước Mắm Chấm*; see Chapter 6) and Sriracha hot sauce (to taste). Fill the sandwich with lettuce, sliced cucumber, Vietnamese herbs (such as perilla leaves, Vietnamese mint, and Thai basil), thin slices of jalapeño, and the condiment(s) of your choice, such as Pickled Carrots and Daikon (*Đồ Chua*; see Chapter 6). Garnish with 2 sprigs of cilantro. Close the sandwich tightly.

N ước M ắ m C hấ m For added sweetness, you could replace the water required for the Fish Sauce (*Nước Mắm Chấm*) recipe (Chapter 6) with pure freshly pressed sugarcane juice and add 1 tablespoon freshly grated ginger. The resulting sauce, which is called *nước mắm gừng*, is especially good in this recipe.

CRAB CAKES

Nem Cua Biển

YIELDS ABOUT 60 PIECES

Nem Cua Biển are a specialty from Hải Phòng in northern Vietnam. They're similar to Eggrolls (*Chả Giò*) (which translates to "rolls"), except they're flavored with kohlrabi, bean thread noodles, and crabmeat, they're square-shaped, and they're wrapped in beer-brushed rice papers. Get ready for mouth-watering, deep-fried gems, but be warned: They disappear fast because they're so delicious!

1 whole fresh crab (see sidebar)

1–1½ cups water

1 pound veal, freshly ground (or pork)

2 teaspoons baking powder

¼ cup green onions, finely chopped

2 teaspoons freshly grated ginger

½ teaspoon salt

1 teaspoon black pepper, freshly ground

1 (2-ounce) package dried bean thread noodles

1 yam

½ cup peanut oil (or any neutral oil), as needed

1 carrot, peeled and finely chopped

1 kohlrabi (*su hào*), peeled and chopped, or jicama

½ cup wood ear mushrooms, thinly sliced

½ cup shiitake mushrooms (*nấm hương*), finely chopped

2 teaspoons mushroom seasoning salt (*bột nêm*) (or regular salt)

3 shallots, or store-bought dried fried shallots

3 tablespoons canola oil, or as needed

2 egg whites

1 (6.8-ounce) bottle beer, as needed

2 packages rice paper disks (*bánh tráng*)

1. **Preparing the crab:** Clean the crab, brush the abdominal flaps and in between the claws, and rinse thoroughly. Place in a pot, add about 1–1½ cups of water, and bring to a boil for about 10–15 minutes (count approximately 8 minutes per pound). Transfer to an ice-water bath for about 3 minutes to stop the cooking process. Drain and discard all liquid. Remove and discard the abdominal flaps (the triangle-shaped tail). Lift and separate the back fin along with the rest of the claws: Place a spoon at the bottom of the crab, where the opening from the abdominal flaps are located, and use the stem of the spoon as a lever to lift the back fin. Remove and discard the "lungs" (also known as devil's fingers); they have a spongy texture and are inedible. Gently remove the crabmeat from the back fins (the inner chambers are filled with meat). Gently crack the claws using a meat tenderizer mallet, remove the meat from the claws, and place all the crabmeat in a large mixing bowl. Set aside.

2. **Preparing the meat:** In a large bowl, combine the ground meat, 1 teaspoon baking powder, green onions, and ginger. Season with salt and pepper. Cover with plastic wrap and refrigerate for at least 2 hours.

3. **For the dried bean thread noodles:** Place the whole package of dried bean thread noodles in a bowl, removing and discarding the little threads. Soak the noodles in cold water for 30–40 minutes (up to 1 hour, depending on the brand), then drain. Chop into 1" pieces. Set aside.

4. **For the yam:** Peel and shred the yam. Place in a large bowl. Fill the bowl with ice water (it should barely cover the shredded yam). Let sit for about 15 minutes, then drain all the liquid. Pat dry. In a frying pan, add about 2 tablespoons of peanut oil. Sprinkle about 4–5 tablespoons yam (working in several batches) evenly into the pan. Do not stir. Cook for at least 3–4 minutes, until one side is slightly fried and lightly golden. Flip the yam using chopsticks. When it's crisp on the second side, transfer to a platter lined with paper towels.

5. **Flavoring the *nem cua* filling:** Add yam, carrots, chopped kohlrabi, bean thread noodles, and wood ear and shiitake mushrooms to the meat mixture. Sprinkle with mushroom seasoning salt. Mix gently. Refrigerate the mixture until you're ready to wrap the *nem cua*.

6. **Frying the shallots:** Peel and slice the shallots. In a large nonstick pan, heat 2 tablespoons canola oil. Working in batches (for extra crispness), add the shallots and fry over high heat for 5 minutes until crisp and golden brown. Transfer to a platter lined with paper towels. Add more oil between batches if necessary.

7. **Making _nem cua_ filling:** Add the fried shallots, crabmeat, and egg whites to the filling made in the previous step. Mix until combined.

8. **Key to proper seasoning:** In a small pan, heat about 1 teaspoon of oil. Add about 1 tablespoon of the filling mixture. Cook for 3 minutes. Taste and season with more salt and pepper if necessary.

9. **Moistening the rice paper disks:** Combine 1 teaspoon baking powder and beer in a shallow bowl or dish. Mix well. Fold a paper towel several times to create a thick sponge. Dip it in the beer mixture and brush both sides of a rice paper disk. Rice paper disks are breakable at first and flimsy once wet, so don't drench them in liquid or they'll become a gluey mess. Transfer to a flat platter lined with towels. Moisten 6 disks at a time. Cover the moistened disks with another towel. Wait about 1 or 2 minutes, then start wrapping. Make sure the remaining disks are covered while you roll each _nem cua_.

10. **Shaping _nem cua_:** Place about 1–2 tablespoons of the _nem cua_ filling at the center of a disk. Carefully fold opposite side flaps over the filling and then fold up the bottom flap facing away from you, forming a square purse shape. The _nem cua_ shouldn't be folded too tightly or it will burst, but also not too loosely, or it will fall apart while frying. If the rice paper disk is moistened properly, it should easily stick and fold. Repeat until all the ingredients are used, keeping the _nem cua_ covered as you work. Once all the _nem cua_ are done, you can cover the platter with plastic wrap and store them in the refrigerator until you're ready to fry them.

11. **Frying time:** Pour the oil into a large frying pan to a depth of at least 1½". Bring to medium-high heat. Make sure the pan is deep enough so there is enough room to add the _nem cua_ without the oil overflowing. Place the _nem cua_ in the hot oil one at a time, seam side down, to prevent splattering. When you see bubbles, reduce the heat to medium-low to prevent the rolls from burning. As soon as each _nem cua_ turns slightly golden, rotate it. When the _nem cua_ are evenly golden all the way around, remove from the pan and place on paper towels to drain the oil. They should be nice and crispy.

12. **Sandwich assembly:** Use 1 baguette per serving. Cut lengthwise into the baguette and remove some of the crumb. Spread a thin layer of butter on one side and Lime Mayonnaise (_Sốt Ma Dô Ne_; see Chapter 6) on the other. Cut each _nem cua_ in half crosswise. Add halved pieces to the sandwich. Drizzle the inside of the baguette with Fish Sauce (_Nước Mắm Chấm_; see Chapter 6) and Sriracha hot sauce (to taste). Add thin slices of jalapeño, a generous amount of shredded lettuce, and the condiment(s) of your choice, such as Pickled Carrots and Daikon (_Đồ Chua_; see Chapter 6). Garnish with 2 sprigs of cilantro. Close the sandwich tightly.

CRAB For shorter preparation time, you could use frozen or canned crabmeat. Simply blanch the crabmeat in boiling water and pat dry before adding to the meat mixture. That way the crab is thoroughly rinsed, free from any impurities, and smells fresh. You could also buy already cooked whole crabs from a supermarket or fish market, where they'll usually clean and crack them for you.

GRAPEFRUIT AND SHRIMP SALAD

Gỏi Bưởi Ngó Sen

YIELDS 6 SERVINGS

This very refreshing seafood salad consists of flavorful shrimp (*tôm*), cucumber, chile peppers, and grapefruit. The whole mixture is topped with cilantro, fragrant Vietnamese herbs, lotus (*ngó sen*), and roasted peanuts for crunch.

1 cucumber

1½ tablespoons salt

3 shallots, or store-bought dried fried shallots

3 tablespoons canola oil, or as needed

½ jicama

1 pound raw medium shrimp, thawed

1 quart water

2 tablespoons palm sugar (or granulated sugar), freshly grated

2 tablespoons rice vinegar

¼ teaspoon red chile powder

¼ teaspoon black pepper, freshly cracked

2 grapefruits

1 teaspoon sesame oil

1 red Thai chile pepper, stemmed, seeded, and finely chopped

½ cup pickled lotus roots, drained, rinsed, and halved diagonally

Juice of 1 lime, freshly squeezed

2 tablespoons perilla leaves (*tía tô*)

3 tablespoons Vietnamese spicy coriander (*rau răm*)

3 tablespoons cilantro, chopped

2 tablespoons Vietnamese mint

2 tablespoons Thai basil

1. **Preparing the cucumber:** Cut the cucumber in half lengthwise. Using a spoon, remove the seeds, which will create a cavity. Slice the cucumber 1" thick. Place a cooling rack on a cookie sheet, and place the cucumber slices on top. Sprinkle ½ teaspoon of the salt on both sides and let sit for at least 30 minutes. Pat dry with a kitchen towel. Cut into 1" matchsticks. Set aside.

2. **Frying the shallots:** Peel and slice the shallots. In a large nonstick pan, heat 2 tablespoons oil. Working in batches (for extra crispness), add the shallots and fry over high heat for 5 minutes until crisp and golden brown. Transfer to a platter lined with paper towels. Add more oil between batches if necessary.

3. **For the jicama:** Peel and slice horizontally into ½"-thick pieces. Add 1 tablespoon oil to the pan used for the shallots. Over high heat, fry the jicama slices until golden brown. Drain on paper towels. Once they're cool enough to handle, cut the pieces into very thin strips. Set aside.

4. **Preparing the shrimp:** If necessary, remove and discard the shrimp heads. Combine 1 quart water, 1 tablespoon of the palm sugar, 2 tablespoons rice vinegar, ¼ teaspoon chile powder, and 1 tablespoon fried shallots in a saucepan. Bring to a boil. Add the shrimp to the liquid (the color of the shrimp will change as they're cooked) for about 2–3 minutes. Add ½ teaspoon of the salt. Check doneness of the shrimp; they should be firm and white with shades of orange. Drain the cooked shrimp, reserving the liquid for the dipping sauce. Once they're cool enough to handle, carefully shell (make sure to remove the tip of the tail as well; this part is very delicate) and remove the black vein of the shrimp using a sharp hook-like paring knife. Cut them in half lengthwise. Sprinkle with black pepper.

5. **Segmenting the grapefruit:** Peel the fruit and divide it in half. Remove the membrane wall on one side around a segment. Apply a little pressure on the segment with your thumb to separate the segment along the next membrane (you could also use a paring knife, but don't cut the fruit; use the knife as a separator). Free the segment and gently pull it away from the fruit so it remains intact, removing all the membrane. Repeat and remove the rest of the segments. This technique releases the flesh and spills less juice. Transfer the grapefruit segments with as much juice as possible

into a bowl. Season with salt and white pepper. Drizzle with sesame oil. Cover well until all the segments are coated with the dressing.

6. **Assembly time:** In a mixing bowl, combine the jicama, shrimp, red chile peppers, lotus root, lime juice, remaining shallots, and cucumbers. Toss well. Add the chopped *tô* (perilla), *rau răm* leaves (Vietnamese coriander), cilantro, mint, and basil. (To prevent the herbs from bruising and darkening, tear the leaves with your fingers at the very last minute and lightly toss them into the salad.) Decorate with more shrimp on top. Immediately fill the sandwiches with the seafood salad.

7. **Sandwich assembly:** Use 1 baguette per serving. Cut lengthwise into the baguette and remove some of the crumb. Spread a thin layer of butter on one side. Fill the sandwich with the seafood salad. Drizzle the inside of the baguette with Fish Sauce (*Nước Mắm Chấm*; see Chapter 6). Add thin slices of jalapeño, a generous number of grapefruit segments, and the condiment(s) of your choice, such as Pickled Carrots and Daikon (*Đồ Chua*) and Pickled Bean Sprouts (*Dưa Giá Với Hẹ Trái Táo Xanh*) (see Chapter 6 for both condiments). Sprinkle with coarsely crushed peanuts and garnish with 2 sprigs of cilantro. Close the sandwich tightly.

JICAMA Jicama (*củ sắn* in Vietnamese) is a large, sweet, firm root vegetable that, when fried, is used in vegetarian Vietnamese cuisine to imitate juicy pork fat and pork skin. It's crunchy like an apple and filling like a potato. You can find it in most supermarket produce sections.

CHAPTER 6

SIDES AND CONDIMENTS

Pickles and mayo from the supermarket may be common sandwich accompaniments, but there is nothing common in the variety of condiments used in Vietnamese cuisine. Exotic ingredients like pickled daikon, papaya, and mango; and condiments like *nước mắm chấm* (fish sauce) and lime mayonnaise are so flavorful and out of the ordinary that they will find their way into your more "traditional" sandwiches. Vietnamese sauces and pickles are typically prepared fresh and used quickly, so they don't last very long. That's not really a problem though, because they are so versatile and easy to use. In this section you'll also find side dishes, the most popular of which are Eggrolls (*Chả Giò*) and Vietnamese Spring Rolls (*Gỏi Cuốn*). This chapter provides the essential ingredients and recipes you'll need to take your sandwiches from ordinary to extraordinary. Your creations will rival the cuisine found in traditional *bánh mì* shops!

FISH SAUCE

Nước Mắm Chấm

YIELDS ABOUT ½ CUP

Most Vietnamese meals revolve around an intensely flavored dipping sauce called *Nước Mắm Chấm*. The main ingredient is fermented fish sauce, which is rich in calcium and salt. This very pungent sauce is a common flavoring in Vietnamese cuisine.

6 tablespoons water
6 tablespoons cane sugar
½ red Thai chile pepper, or to taste
3 tablespoons rice vinegar
1 lemon, freshly squeezed
1 clove garlic, finely minced
¼ cup fish sauce (*nước mắm*)

1. **Dissolving the sugar:** Bring 6 tablespoons water to a near-boil. Add and dissolve the sugar. Let the liquid cool to room temperature. It's important that you wait until the water is completely cool to add the rest of the ingredients; otherwise, you'll end up cooking some of them.

2. **Preparing the chile:** Stem the chile. Using a paring knife, cut a 2"–3" slit in the pepper. For less heat, remove the seeds (be sure not to rub your eyes after touching chile pepper seeds). Finely chop the pepper and set aside.

3. **Assembly time:** Add the rice vinegar and lemon juice to the cooled sugar mixture. Mix in the garlic and red chile pepper. Let all the flavors combine for at least 30 minutes. Stir in the fish sauce. You can store the dipping sauce in the refrigerator for up to 10 days.

VEGETARIAN DIPPING SAUCE

Nước Chấm Chay

YIELDS ABOUT ½ CUP

Nước Chấm Chay is a great alternative to *Nước Mắm Chấm* not only for vegetarians but also for those who find the traditional fish sauce a bit too pungent. In Vietnam both this sauce and its fish-based equivalent are as common on the dinner table as a salt shaker is in the West.

½ cup water
6 tablespoons cane sugar
½ red Thai chile pepper, or to taste
3 limes, freshly squeezed
1 clove garlic, finely minced
¼ cup dark soy sauce

1. **Dissolving the sugar:** Bring ½ cup water to a near-boil. Add and dissolve the sugar. Let the liquid cool to room temperature. It's important that you wait until the water is completely cool to add the rest of the ingredients; otherwise, you'll end up cooking some of them.

2. **Preparing the chile:** Stem the chile. Using a paring knife, cut a 2"–3" slit in the pepper. For less heat, remove the seeds (be sure not to rub your eyes after touching chile pepper seeds). Finely chop the pepper and set aside.

3. **Assembly time:** Add the lime juice to the cooled sugar mixture. Mix in the garlic and red chile pepper. Let all the flavors combine for at least 30 minutes. Stir in the soy sauce. You can store the dipping sauce in the refrigerator for up to 10 days.

PICKLED GARLIC

Tỏi Chua Ngọt

YIELDS 6 SERVINGS

Pickled garlic is a typical relish served with a Vietnamese meal. Since some of the garlic's pungent taste and aroma diffuse into the pickling liquid, pickled garlic is usually very mild.

1 head garlic
1 red Thai chile, to taste
2 tablespoons granulated sugar
⅓ cup rice vinegar
2 cups water
1 teaspoon salt

1. **Preparing the garlic:** Trim the ends of the cloves of garlic and peel them. Cut them in half lengthwise.

2. **Preparing the chile:** Stem the chile. Using a paring knife, cut a 2"–3" slit in the pepper. For less heat, remove the seeds (be sure not to rub your eyes after touching chile pepper seeds). Finely chop the chile.

3. **Making the brine:** In a small saucepan, combine the sugar, vinegar, and 1 cup of the water. Bring to a near-boil. Make sure the temperature doesn't exceed 104°F. Add salt and 1 cup cold water; stir well. Let cool to room temperature.

4. **Assembly time:** Place the garlic and chopped chile in a Mason jar. Cover with the brine. Cap the jar and let infuse in a cool place for 3–4 days. Check the garlic after 3 days. You can store the pickles up to 2 weeks in the refrigerator.

LIME MAYONNAISE

Sốt Ma Dô Ne

YIELDS ½ CUP

A *bánh mì* wouldn't be complete without mayonnaise; it's almost always generously spread on one side of the baguette. It typically has a thinner texture than French mayonnaise. The secret behind its distinctive taste is a simple ingredient: lime.

1 egg yolk
¼ teaspoon rice vinegar
1 teaspoon honey, optional
1 teaspoon Dijon mustard
⅓–½ cup vegetable oil, as needed (see sidebar)
Juice of 1 lime with pulp, freshly squeezed
¼ teaspoon sea salt (or regular salt)
⅛ teaspoon red chile powder, optional

Note: All the ingredients should be at room temperature. For optimum results, the oil should be slightly warmed (70°F).

1. **Making the mayonnaise:** In a glass bowl, whisk the egg yolk (you can also use a food processor or a blender instead of whisking by hand). Add rice vinegar, honey (if using), and Dijon mustard. Whisk continuously while very slowly adding ⅓ cup oil a little at a time until fully combined. It's essential that you add the oil slowly; the mayonnaise will not turn out well if you rush this step. Whisk until emulsified, either by hand or with a blender or food processor. Thin the sauce with lime juice. Stir until the color is uniform.

2. **Seasoning:** Season with salt and chile powder (if using). Feel free to spice it up with Sriracha hot sauce, or give it a more intense yellow color with turmeric, or add finely minced Pickled Garlic (*Tỏi Chua Ngọt*; see recipe in this chapter). Let sit at room temperature for no more than 1 hour before serving or refrigerate and store up to 10 days.

PICKLED MANGO

Gỏi Xoài Xanh

YIELDS 6 SERVINGS

If you aren't too keen on sour pickles, these less-common green mango pickles may be the perfect condiment for your sandwich. They have a heavenly flavor and texture: slightly sour but also salty, sweet yet spicy, with a slight crunch.

2 red Thai bird chiles, or to taste

¼ cup grated palm sugar (or granulated sugar)

½ teaspoon salt

Juice of 4 limes, freshly squeezed

5 carrots

2 green mangoes

2 tablespoons *củ kiệu* (white root onions), thinly sliced

2 tablespoons rice vinegar

2 tablespoons boiling water

1 teaspoon soy sauce

2 cloves Pickled Garlic (*Tỏi Chua Ngọt*; see recipe in this chapter), finely minced

1 tablespoon cilantro, chopped

¼ cup Vietnamese mint, coarsely chopped

½ teaspoon white pepper, freshly cracked using a mortar and pestle

1. **For the chiles:** Wash and stem the Thai bird chiles. Pat dry with a paper towel. For less heat, remove and discard the seeds from the chiles. The seeds are attached to a ribbed membrane, which is where most of the heat lies. Finely chop the chiles.

2. **For the chile salt:** In a mortar and pestle, combine 2 teaspoons of the sugar, salt, and red chiles. Drizzle in a few drops of lime juice and allow the mixture to macerate for a few hours. The salt will turn a pinkish color.

3. **Preparing the carrots and mangoes:** Trim the carrots on both ends. Peel the carrots and cut lengthwise into long thin strips using a vegetable peeler, then cut the strips into about 5" lengths. You could also slice the carrots with a mandoline. Peel the mangoes and cut into long, thin strips with a vegetable peeler until you reach the stone of the fruit. If the strips are too wide, you might want to cut them lengthwise, using a sharp knife. Place the carrots, green mangoes, and *củ kiệu* in a large mixing bowl. Sprinkle with the chile salt. Drizzle with 1 tablespoon of the lime juice and vinegar. Toss well. Let sit for 15–30 minutes.

4. ***Gỏi* sauce (salad dressing):** In a bowl, dissolve the remaining sugar in 2 tablespoons of boiling water. Let the water cool to room temperature. Add the remaining lime juice and soy sauce. Mix in the pickled garlic.

5. **Assembly time:** Drain and discard the macerating liquid from the pickled vegetables (carrots, mango, and *củ kiệu*). Add the *gỏi* dressing to the vegetables. Toss thoroughly. Set aside for about 10 minutes. Drain and discard about half of the liquid; otherwise the salad will be too watery. When you're ready to serve, add the chopped cilantro and mint. Toss well. Season with more soy sauce (if needed) and sprinkle with freshly cracked white pepper. Serve immediately.

PICKLED MANGO: *Gỏi Xoài Xanh*

PICKLED ASPARAGUS

Gỏi Măng Tây

YIELDS 6 SERVINGS

Gỏi Măng Tây literally translates to "French bamboo shoots" in Vietnamese. What are French bamboo shoots, you ask? Asparagus! They provide a different texture for this type of raw salad since only the young shoots are eaten. The asparagus should be carefully peeled for optimum tenderness.

1 (16-ounce) bunch thin, young, white asparagus

1 teaspoon salt

3 tablespoons granulated sugar

2 tablespoons boiling water

Juice of 4 limes, freshly squeezed

2 teaspoons ponzu soy sauce, to taste

2 cloves Pickled Garlic (*Tỏi Chua Ngọt*; see recipe in this chapter) or fresh garlic, crushed and finely minced

1 red Thai bird chile, stemmed, seeded, and finely chopped

2 tablespoons *củ kiệu* (white root onions), thinly sliced

2 tablespoons cilantro, coarsely chopped

2 tablespoons Thai basil, torn into small pieces

½ teaspoon white pepper, freshly ground

1. **Preparing the asparagus:** Trim about 1" from the root ends of the asparagus if necessary (depending on how young they are). Using a vegetable peeler, peel the asparagus, then cut them into long, thin strips. Be very gentle; white asparagus is very delicate and can break easily. Add to a mixing bowl. Sprinkle with salt to draw out moisture and 1 teaspoon sugar. Toss well. Let sit for about 5–10 minutes. Drain through a fine mesh colander. Discard the liquid. Pat the asparagus dry with paper towels.

2. **Making *gỏi* sauce (salad dressing):** In a bowl, dissolve the remaining sugar in 2 tablespoons of boiling water. Let the water cool to room temperature. Add the lime juice and soy sauce. Mix in the garlic and red Thai chile.

3. **Assembly time:** Pat dry the asparagus one more time. Add the *gỏi* dressing. To make sure the salad isn't overdressed, add the *củ kiệu* and a few tablespoons of dressing at a time. Toss thoroughly. Set aside for about 5 minutes. Drain and discard about half of the liquid; otherwise the salad will be too watery. When you're ready to serve, add the chopped cilantro and Thai basil. Toss well. Sprinkle with white pepper.

PICKLED PAPAYA

Gỏi Đu Đủ

YIELDS 6 SERVINGS

This unique Vietnamese salad is often paired with savory, sweet, and spicy Vietnamese beef jerky (*khô bò*; see Beef Jerky and Papaya Salad, Chapter 4), which is well-balanced by the natural sweetness of the shredded green papaya (*đu đủ*). It looks as good as it tastes; the colors are striking and inviting.

1½ pounds green papaya, shredded

½ daikon radish, shredded

1 tablespoon sea salt (or regular salt)

4 tablespoons granulated sugar

¼ cup boiling water

Juice of 2 lemons, freshly squeezed

¼ cup cold water

2 teaspoons ponzu soy sauce, or to taste

2 cloves Pickled Garlic (*Tỏi Chua Ngọt*; see recipe in this chapter) or fresh garlic, crushed and finely minced

1 red Thai bird chile, seeded and finely chopped (optional)

3 tablespoons Thai basil leaves, stems removed

1 tablespoon Vietnamese mint

½ teaspoon white pepper, freshly cracked using a mortar and pestle

Sriracha hot sauce (optional)

1. **Preparing the papaya and daikon radish:** Combine the papaya and daikon in a mixing bowl. Add a scant teaspoon water; sprinkle with salt and 1 teaspoon of the sugar. Let sit for 5–10 minutes. Drain using a fine mesh colander. Rinse the shredded mixture and place it in a piece of cheesecloth. Remove as much excess water as possible. Pat dry with paper towels.

2. ***Gỏi* sauce (salad dressing):** In a bowl, dissolve the remaining sugar in ¼ cup of boiling water. Let the water cool to room temperature. Add the lemon juice, ¼ cup of cold water, and soy sauce. Mix in the garlic, salt, and red Thai bird chile (if using).

3. **Assembly time:** Pat dry the pickled vegetables one more time. Add the *gỏi* dressing. To make sure the salad isn't drenched in dressing, add a few tablespoons at a time. Toss thoroughly. Set aside for 10 minutes. Drain and discard about half of the liquid; otherwise the salad will be too watery. When you're ready to serve, add the chopped basil and mint. Season with white pepper. Toss well. Season with more soy sauce (if needed). Serve with Sriracha hot sauce on the side for those who like the dish spicy.

PICKLED BEAN SPROUTS

Dưa Giá Với Hẹ Trái Táo Xanh

YIELDS 6 SERVINGS

Bean sprouts are usually sold in large 1-pound packages. If you don't want to waste them, search no more. Here's a recipe for *Dưa Giá Với Hẹ Trái Táo Xanh*, which literally translates to "pickled bean sprouts with Chinese chives and green apples." However, the apples (*trái táo*) and Chinese chives (*hẹ*) are optional.

6 tablespoons grated palm sugar

⅔ cup rice vinegar

4 cups water

2 teaspoons salt

1 (4") piece ginger

1 red Thai bird chile, seeded and finely chopped

1 pound bean sprouts, rinsed

½ bunch Chinese chives (*hẹ*), cut into 2" pieces (optional)

2 cloves Pickled Garlic (*Tỏi Chua Ngọt*; see recipe in this chapter) or fresh garlic, crushed and finely minced

1 green apple (optional)

½ teaspoon white pepper, freshly cracked using a mortar and pestle

1. **For the brine:** In a small saucepan, combine the sugar, vinegar, and 2 cups of the water. Bring to a near-boil. Make sure the temperature doesn't exceed 104°F. Add salt and 2 cups cold water; stir well. Let the brine cool to room temperature.

2. **Preparing the ginger:** Clean the ginger and peel it with the edge of a spoon. Slice and then cut it into julienne strips. Set aside.

3. **Preparing the chile:** Stem the chile. Using a paring knife, cut a 2"–3" slit in the pepper. For less heat, remove the seeds (be sure not to rub your eyes after touching chile pepper seeds). Finely chop the chile.

4. **Assembly time:** Pat the bean sprouts dry. In a large mixing bowl, combine the bean sprouts, Chinese chives (if using), chiles, ginger, and pickled garlic. Add the brine. Toss thoroughly. Set aside for about 10 minutes. When you're ready to serve, core the green apple (if using). Slice the apple and then cut each slice into matchstick-size pieces. Add to the pickled vegetables. Toss well. Drain and discard the liquid; otherwise the salad will be too watery. Sprinkle with freshly cracked white pepper. Serve immediately.

PICKLED VIETNAMESE CABBAGE

Dưa Muối

YIELDS 6 SERVINGS

Pickled cabbage is absolutely delicious and goes with almost any meal. Cabbage, very simple seasoning, and a good bit of patience are the only things necessary here. It takes a few days for the cabbage to ferment, and then it's ready to enjoy.

1 lemon
2 pounds green mustard (Vietnamese cabbage)
½ cup sea salt (or regular salt)
2 tablespoons sugar
1 teaspoon red chile flakes
½ cup rice vinegar (or regular white vinegar)
1 teaspoon sesame oil
2 quarts water
1 white onion (milder in flavor than yellow onion), sliced
1 (1") chunk fresh ginger, peeled and sliced
4 cloves garlic, crushed

1. **Preparing the lemon:** Cut the lemon in half; juice one half and slice the rest.

2. **Preparing the cabbage:** Separate all the leaves from the root, which is fibrous and tough to eat. Wash the cabbage thoroughly under cold running water. Place all the leaves in a large bowl, sprinkle with ¼ cup of the salt, and barely cover with water and the lemon juice. Soak for about 30 minutes. Rinse and cut each leaf in half lengthwise, then cut each piece in thirds.

3. **Making the pickling brine:** In a small bowl, combine remaining ¼ cup salt, 1 tablespoon of the sugar, red chile flakes, rice vinegar, and sesame oil. Whisk well. Adjust seasoning; you can add up to ½–1 tablespoons of sugar altogether depending on the acidity of the vinegar. Add 2 quarts of water. Stir well.

4. **Assembly time:** In another bowl, combine the onion, ginger, and lemon slices. Toss well. In a large, clean crock or glass jar, stack and tightly pack the cabbage leaves, alternating with the combined lemon, garlic cloves, onion, and ginger slices. Using a funnel, cover the leaves with the pickling brine. Weight the vegetables down using a heavy small plate. Cap the jar and allow to rest for 3–4 days at room temperature (not to exceed 70°F). The fermenting period varies with the temperature of the room. Check the pickles after 3 days. If you see bubbles, they should be ready. Once you achieve the desired amount of fermentation, which should take no longer than 5 days, you can store the pickles up to 2 weeks in the refrigerator.

PICKLED CARROTS AND DAIKON

Đồ Chua

YIELDS 3 (4-OUNCE) MASON JARS

Pickled carrots and daikon are a substitute for French cornichons in the traditional *jambon-beurre* (French ham and butter baguette sandwich). After the colonial period, only wealthy people could afford imported French goods. The spontaneous response was to replicate the French dishes as closely as possible. The Vietnamese sought out and replaced the costly French ingredients they adored with what was available inland, and *đồ chua* became a signature element in *bánh mì*.

1 white onion, peeled, halved, and sliced
1½ teaspoons salt
½–¾ cup white vinegar, to taste
2 small carrots
1 large daikon
1½ tablespoons granulated sugar

1. **Preparing the onion:** Place the sliced onion in a large bowl. Sprinkle with 1 teaspoon of the salt. Let sit for about 1 hour. Press out and drain. Rinse in a water bath, then drain again and pat dry.

2. **Preparing the vegetables:** Dissolve the remaining salt in the vinegar. Peel the carrots and daikon and shred them: Make ribbons using a vegetable peeler, then cut into very thin strips using a sharp knife. Cut the shreds into 3" pieces. You could also slice the vegetables with a mandoline, then julienne them using a sharp knife. Do not use a grater blade on a food processor for this process; it would make the vegetables mushy. Place the carrots and daikon in a bowl. Sprinkle with sugar. Drizzle with the salted vinegar. Toss well. Let sit for about 15 minutes. Add the onions and mix well. Drain the vegetables, reserving as much liquid as possible.

3. **Assembly time:** Fill Mason jars with the carrots, daikon, and onions. Divide the salted vinegar equally among 3 jars. Add water to fill the jars. Cover with the lids and store in the refrigerator for at least 1 hour. For optimal flavor, you should allow about 4 days before opening the jars.

BEET PICKLES

Củ Cải Đường Muối Chua

YIELDS 1 (1-QUART) JAR (SERVES 6)

Pickled beets are delicious condiments for *bánh mì*. They add crunch and natural sweetness. The preparation is so easy, and they make a perfect hostess gift!

1 pound beets
2 quarts water
1 tablespoon salt
½ cup granulated sugar
1 whole red Thai chile pepper, stemmed
1 cup rice vinegar
2 cinnamon sticks
¾ teaspoon cumin seeds, lightly toasted
¾ teaspoon coriander seeds
¾ teaspoon mustard seeds
 1 red onion, thickly sliced
1 (1") chunk fresh ginger, peeled and sliced

1. **Cooking the beets:** Scrub the beets under running water. Peel and trim off a little piece of each beet from the end of the root. Place the beets in a small saucepan and add just enough cold water to cover the bottom ⅓ of the beets. Bring to a boil, then lower the heat to a gentle simmer. Cook for 20–30 minutes until softened, depending on their size. A good way to check is to poke the beets with a paring knife (it should easily pierce the beets, but they shouldn't fall apart). Check the liquid periodically and add more water if necessary. Drain the water and allow to cool.

2. **Making the brine:** In a small saucepan, combine the salt, sugar, red chile, rice vinegar, cinnamon, cumin, coriander seeds, and mustard seeds. Add 1 cup water. Stir well. Bring to a boil.

3. **Assembly time:** Slice the beets thinly. Arrange layers of beets in a jar, alternating with the red onions and ginger slices. Using a funnel, cover the beets with the pickling brine. Weigh the vegetables down using a small heavy plate. Partially cover the jar and let cool to room temperature. Cap the jar and store for 3–7 days in the refrigerator. Usually 5 days is the right amount of time until the pickles taste right. Check the pickles after 3 days.

VIETNAMESE SPRING ROLLS

Gỏi Cuốn

YIELDS 6 SERVINGS

Spring rolls are the perfect finger food (*món ăn chơi*); they're usually served in halves as appetizers with Hoisin Peanut Dipping Sauce (*Tương Gỏi Cuốn*) on the side (see sidebar). Shrimp, pork, rice noodles, and fragrant Vietnamese herbs are wrapped in tapioca disks called *bánh tráng mỏng*. They're rolled so the shrimp are still visible, for an appealing look.

1 tablespoon canola oil

1 small white onion, thinly sliced

½ pork tenderloin (about ¾ pound)

¼ teaspoon red chile powder

1 tablespoon freshly grated palm sugar (or granulated sugar)

1½ teaspoons salt

2 tablespoons white vinegar

2 dozen raw medium shrimp, thawed

6 *hẹ* (Chinese chives), for garnish

1 dozen lettuce leaves

1 cup Vietnamese mint, stemmed

1 cup Thai basil, stemmed

½ cucumber

12 *bánh tráng mỏng* disks (tapioca disks)

5 ounces thin rice vermicelli noodles, boiled and drained

1 cup bean sprouts (optional)

2 cups Hoisin Peanut Dipping Sauce (see sidebar)

Chopped roasted peanuts (for garnish)

Sriracha hot sauce (optional)

1. **Preparing the meat:** Heat the oil in a large pot. Add the white onion and pan-fry for 6–8 minutes until crisp and golden. Add water to the pot to a depth of 3". Bring to a boil and cook the onions for about 5 minutes. Add the meat to the onion broth. Add more water if not fully covered (the level should be about 1" above the meat). Bring back to a boil, then lower the heat to medium-low. Cook for 15 minutes. Add red chile powder, sugar, 1 teaspoon salt, and vinegar. Cook 2–3 more minutes (until the meat is no longer pink in the center). Remove the whole piece of meat from the pot. Let it cool a bit until you can handle it without discomfort. Thinly slice the meat crosswise. Reserve the broth for cooking the shrimp.

2. **Preparing the shrimp:** Remove and discard the shrimp heads if necessary. Bring the broth back to a boil. Dip the shrimp into the liquid for 2–3 minutes. Once the shrimp turn slightly opaque, add ½ teaspoon salt. Check doneness of the shrimp; they should be firm and white, with shades of orange. Drain the cooked shrimp, reserving the liquid for the dipping sauce. Once the shrimp are cool enough to handle, carefully shell (make sure to remove the tip of the tail as well; this part is very delicate). Devein the shrimp (remove the thin black vein) using a sharp hook-like paring knife, then halve lengthwise.

3. **For the herbs (*rau thơm*):** Wash and drain the Chinese chives with a salad spinner. Set aside. Repeat the same procedure with the lettuce, mint, and basil. Remove as much liquid as possible from all the greens.

4. **Preparing the cucumber:** Cut the cucumber into 2"–3" matchsticks (match the length to the size of your tapioca disks).

5. **Preparing the tapioca disks:** Fill a saucepan with water. Bring the water to a boil. Let cool a bit. Transfer to a large bowl. It's important that the water isn't too hot. Fold a paper towel several times to create a thick sponge. Dip it in the hot water and brush both sides of a tapioca disk. Remember, tapioca disks are a lot more delicate than rice paper; you don't want too much water. Place the disk on a flat surface. Wait about 1 or 2 minutes. The tapioca disk should be soft and damp but not too wet. Dip 4 tapioca disks at a time, then start wrapping.

6. **Shaping the spring rolls:** Place a softened tapioca disk on a flat surface. Arrange the halved shrimp on the disk, so they're still visible once the rolls are wrapped. Start about 1½" from the bottom edge of the disk, so the roll won't burst when it's wrapped (don't overstuff the rolls as you add the toppings). Top with lettuce, mint, basil, rice noodles, and 2 or 3 cucumber "matchsticks." Top with bean sprouts (if using). The finishing touch is 2 long stems of *hẹ*, letting the end and the flower extend out one side of the roll. Carefully fold the side flaps of each sheet over the filling, and then fold up the bottom flap and roll away from you. If the tapioca sheet is moistened properly, it should easily stick and roll. Tuck all the mixture into the wrapper, forming a cigar shape. The flower should stick out and be visible (it's quite fancy to have the flower exposed). Repeat until all the ingredients are used.

7. **Serving suggestion:** The roll should be dipped in Hoisin Peanut Dipping Sauce and sprinkled with crushed peanuts. Sriracha hot sauce can be served on the side.

HOISIN PEANUT DIPPING SAUCE (*TƯƠNG GỎI CUỐN*) In a food processor, combine 1 tablespoon chopped roasted peanuts, 1 tablespoon peanut butter, 2 tablespoons grated palm sugar, ½ cup reserved hot broth with the onions, 1 teaspoon soybean sauce, and ¼ cup hoisin sauce. Pulse until smooth. If it's too thick, you could add more broth to reach the desired consistency. Note: The authentic version calls for liver; you could add mung bean paste for a thick texture.

EGGROLLS

Chả Giò

YIELDS 40–50 ROLLS

Making eggrolls isn't as complicated as it seems. Once you master the art of rolling, you'll see that the preparation is fairly simple. The meat filling is mixed raw and then refrigerated until it's time to fold and fry the eggrolls.

2 pounds pork, freshly ground

1½ teaspoons baking powder

¼ cup leek (green part only), chopped

2 teaspoons grated palm sugar

1 tablespoon freshly grated ginger

½ teaspoon salt

1 teaspoon black pepper, freshly ground

1 (2-ounce) package dried bean thread noodles

½ jicama

½ cup plus 2 tablespoons vegetable oil (or any neutral oil)

1 taro root (optional; see sidebar)

2 white onions, chopped

4 tablespoons fried yellow onions

1 carrot, peeled and finely chopped

½ cup wood ear mushrooms, thinly sliced

2 tablespoons cilantro, chopped

2 teaspoons mushroom seasoning salt (*bột nêm*) (or regular salt)

1 package frozen square eggroll wrappers (30 wrappers)

Frying oil, as needed

1. **Preparing the meat:** In a large bowl, combine the ground pork, baking powder, leek, sugar, and ginger. Season with salt and pepper. Cover with plastic wrap and refrigerate for at least 2 hours.

2. **For the dried bean thread noodles:** Place the whole package of dried bean thread noodles in a bowl. Don't forget to cut and discard the little threads. Soak the noodles in cold water for 30–40 minutes (up to 1 hour, depending on the brand), then drain. Chop into 1" threads. Set aside.

3. **For the jicama:** Peel and slice horizontally into ½"-thick pieces. Heat ½ cup vegetable oil in a large pan and fry the jicama slices until golden brown. Once they are cool enough to handle, cut the pieces into very thin strips, then finely chop them. Set aside.

4. **For the taro (if using):** Peel and shred the taro using a mandoline. Place in a large bowl. Fill the bowl with ice water (it should barely cover the taro root). Let sit for 15 minutes, then drain all the liquid. Pat dry. Add 2 more tablespoons of oil to the pan used for the jicama. Sprinkle 4–5 tablespoons taro (working in several batches) evenly into the pan. Do not stir. Wait for at least 2 minutes until one side is slightly fried and lightly golden. Flip the taro using chopsticks. When the taro is crisp, transfer to a platter lined with paper towels. At that point, the taro isn't fully cooked and will finish cooking when the eggrolls are fried. Continue until all the taro is fried, adding more oil if necessary. Use more paper towels to drain any remaining oil from the taro.

5. **Making eggroll filling:** Remove the ground pork from the refrigerator. Add the taro, jicama, bean thread noodles, white onions, fried onions, carrots, wood ear mushrooms, and cilantro. Sprinkle with mushroom seasoning salt. Mix well. Refrigerate the mixture until you're ready to wrap the eggrolls.

6. **Key to proper seasoning:** In a small pan, heat about 1 teaspoon oil. Add about 1 tablespoon of the filling mixture. Cook for 3 minutes. Taste and season with more salt and pepper if necessary.

7. **Shaping eggrolls:** Fill a small shallow bowl with cold water. Cut the eggroll squares into 2 triangles and separate them. (They're sold in packages of 30 squares that are stuck together, so you will have 60 triangles to work with.) Place

about 1 tablespoon of the eggroll filling at the base of the triangle (the top point of the triangle should face away from you). Moisten one of the corners with your finger and fold it along the base toward the opposite corner so that it just covers the filling. Then roll the wrapper once toward the top corner. Repeat with the other corner along the base. Moisten the exposed top corner with water, then finish rolling.

8. **Storing the eggrolls until frying time:** Once a platter is full of uncooked eggrolls, make sure they're covered with a towel while you roll the rest of the eggrolls. Once done, you can cover the eggrolls with plastic wrap and store them in the refrigerator overnight.

9. **Frying the eggrolls:** Pour oil into a large frying pan to a depth of at least 1½". Make sure the pan is deep enough so there is enough room to add the eggrolls without the oil overflowing. Heat the oil over medium-high heat. Place the eggrolls into the hot oil one at a time, seam side down. When you see bubbles, reduce the heat to medium-low to prevent the rolls from burning. As soon as each eggroll turns slightly golden, rotate it. When the eggrolls are even and golden all the way around, remove from the pan and place on paper towels to drain. They should be golden, crispy, and delicious.

10. **Serving suggestion:** Wrap the eggrolls in lettuce with boiled thin rice vermicelli noodles (called *bún*) and Vietnamese mint, or serve them plain with the sauces on the side as appetizers. Serve with Fish Sauce (*Nước Mắm Chấm;* see Chapter 6) and Sriracha hot sauce on the side.

SAFETY TIPS FOR USING TARO If you want to freeze the eggrolls for future use, omit the taro, which when raw can become toxic during storage. Eggrolls made without taro can be stored up to a month in the freezer.

CHAPTER 7

BEVERAGES

The only rivals to the variety of colors and flavors found in *bánh mì* sandwiches are the Vietnamese beverages that accompany them. *Cà Phê Sữa*, for instance, is a strong, bitter coffee brewed in a special Vietnamese filter and served in a tall glass filled with a copious amount of sweetened condensed milk. Not only is the contrast of black against white quite appealing; it tastes as good as it looks. You'll have a tough time going back to a regular cup of joe after trying this recipe.

Then there are the smoothies, made with fruits such as avocado, honeydew, jackfruit, durian, and sapota. They are exotic, creamy, and deliciously sweet. For something really out of this world, try a glass of Thai basil seed drink. At first glance it may look a little intimidating, but it will quickly become a tasty cure for a hot day.

To end our tour of the typical Vietnamese *bánh mì* shop, you'll find a colorful dessert that is served as a drink (Red Azuki Bean Dessert: *Chè Đậu Đỏ Bánh Lọt*, layered with pandan-flavored jelly noodles and mock pomegranate seeds). Vietnamese people use red beans in many different desserts, and this is a celebrated favorite.

VIETNAMESE-STYLE THAI ICED TEA

Trà Thái

YIELDS 2 SERVINGS

Trà Thái, as the name suggests, is the Vietnamese take on Thai Iced Tea. The traditional version is made with a blend of black tea and Rooibos tea, along with coconut. The authentic coloring agent in *Trà Thái* is crushed tamarind seeds, but you could also use a touch of red food coloring.

1 star anise, slightly crushed

½ teaspoon tamarind seeds (optional), crushed

2½ cups of cold, fresh, filtered water

1 tablespoons loose Thai black tea leaves

2 teaspoons Rooibos tea

2 tablespoons raw cane sugar (optional)

5–6 tablespoons sweetened condensed milk, to taste

2–3 tablespoons coconut milk, to taste

2 cups ice cubes, or crushed ice

⅓ cup half and half, as needed

1. **Preparing the water:** Place the star anise and the tamarind seeds (if using) in a small saucepan and cover with 2½ cups of cold, fresh, filtered water (so there's no taste from the chlorine often present in regular water). Bring the water to a near boil (about 200°F).

2. **Making tea:** The water should be bubbling. Add the black and Rooibos tea to the anise and tamarind-flavored water. Sweeten with sugar. Steep for 12 minutes, no more than that. If black tea is brewed too long or too hot (no more than 200°F), it may develop an unpleasant, bitter, and acidic taste, and degrade the flavor of the drink. Filter the tea through a fine mesh sieve or fine muslin cloth.

3. **Flavoring the Thai tea:** Add the condensed milk and coconut milk; the tea will turn a nice caramel color. Stir well until everything is dissolved. Let the tea completely cool to room temperature. Pour into 2 tall glasses filled with ice cubes. Top with half and half. Stir well.

ADD COLOR TO YOUR TEA   Coarsely ground tamarind seeds imbue the tea with a natural orange color. If you don't have any, you can substitute a hint of red food coloring mixed with twice as much yellow food coloring. You can also add beet powder as a sweetener and natural food coloring.

JACKFRUIT SMOOTHIE

Sinh Tố Mít

YIELDS 4 SERVINGS

Sinh tố trái cây, which literally translates to "fruits with vitamins," is one of the most popular street foods of Vietnam. When the weather is really hot, nothing is more soothing than a smoothie. Jackfruit (*mít* in Vietnamese) with mung beans (*đậu xanh*) is one of the many variations of these Vietnamese drinks. This drink is refreshing, creamy, and because of the mung beans, also fairly filling.

1½ tablespoons mung beans

1½ cups water

⅛ teaspoon salt

4½ cups jackfruit

1 quart ice cubes, crushed

2½ cups soymilk (or any other milk such as coconut milk), as needed (depending on how you like the consistency of your shake)

½–1 cup coconut water

2 tablespoons sweetened condensed milk (or honey), to taste

¼ cup vanilla ice cream

4 fresh mint leaves, for garnish

1. **Making mung bean paste:** Wash and rinse the mung beans thoroughly in several water baths (about three times), discarding any floating or odd-shaped beans. Drain the beans, place them in a small saucepan, and cover with 1½ cups water. Bring to a boil, then lower the heat to a bubbly simmer. Cook for 20–30 minutes until soft, stirring occasionally. After 20 minutes check for doneness; if necessary, add a little more water and continue cooking. When done, the mung beans should be soft when gently pressed between your thumb and index finger. Drain well. Sprinkle with salt.

2. **Assembly time:** Coarsely chop the fruit. In a blender, combine all the ingredients except the mint; blend until very smooth. Add more coconut water until the smoothie reaches the desired consistency. Pour into 4 tall glasses. Garnish with fresh mint leaves.

OTHER FLAVORINGS You could also add your favorite flavorings to this smoothie, such as orange blossom water, ground clove, cinnamon, or licorice.

AVOCADO SMOOTHIE

Sinh Tố Bơ

When you think of avocados, making smoothies is probably not the first idea that comes to mind. That's too bad, because the Vietnamese avocado smoothie, *Sinh Tố Bơ*, is a velvety, sinfully rich drink. All you need are ripe avocados, sweetened condensed milk, soymilk, and a few ice cubes; it's that easy.

4 ripe avocados

Juice of ½ lemon (optional)

1 tablespoon honey (optional)

1 quart ice cubes, crushed

1½ cups soymilk, as needed (depending on how you like the consistency of your shake)

1 cup sweetened condensed milk, to taste

1. **Avocado preparation:** Peel and pit the avocados, then chop them into cubes. Drizzle lemon juice on the avocados to avoid oxidation. Add honey, if you like.

2. **Assembly time:** In a blender, combine all the ingredients until very smooth. Divide into 6 glasses.

AVOCADO SMOOTHIE: *Sinh Tố Bơ*

HONEYDEW BUBBLE MILK TEA WITH TAPIOCA PEARLS

Trà Sữa Dưa Honeydew Trân Châu

YIELDS 6 SERVINGS

Bubble milk tea is a refreshing cold drink that consists of syrup, milk, tea, and often fruit. This version is flavored with green tea (*trà xanh*), honeydew melon (*trái dưa mật tây*), and black tapioca pearls (*hột trân châu*). In just five easy-to-follow steps you can make the trendiest Asian beverage out there.

½ cup large black tapioca pearls (see sidebar)

1 quart plus 2 cups water, divided use

½ cup rock sugar (or granulated sugar)

½ cup Chinese brown sugar (*đường thẻ*) (or regular brown sugar)

1 tablespoon honey

3 green tea bags

1¼ cups sweetened condensed milk, to taste

½ honeydew melon

2 cups soymilk

1 quart shaved ice

1. **For the tapioca pearls:** Wash and rinse the tapioca pearls thoroughly in several water baths (about three times). Discard any floating or odd-shaped pearls. Cover them completely with water. Soak in cold water for about 1 hour. Drain well. Fill a saucepan with 1 quart water and bring to a boil. Add the tapioca pearls and cook for about 20–25 minutes until soft. Stir every now and then so the pearls don't stick to the bottom of the saucepan. Turn off the heat, cover the pan, and let sit for 30 minutes. Once the tapioca pearls are plump and gleaming, drain the pearls and rinse them in lukewarm water.

2. **For the syrup:** Place the rock sugar and the Chinese brown sugar in a saucepan. Add 1 cup water. Bring to a boil, then turn down the heat and let simmer until the sugar is completely dissolved. Remove from the stove, add honey, and allow to cool to room temperature. Add the pearls to the syrup.

3. **For the tea:** Heat 1 cup water until it's hot and bubbling slightly, with steam starting to rise. Add the tea bags and steep them for about 2 minutes, but no longer. Remove and discard the tea bags. Add ½ cup of the condensed milk, stir well, and let cool to room temperature.

4. **For the honeydew:** Remove and discard the skin and seeds of the honeydew and gather 5–6 cups. Place in a blender with the remaining condensed milk and blend into a smooth purée. For a smoother flow, add some of the soymilk. Transfer to a cocktail shaker; add the green tea, remaining soymilk, and shaved ice. Shake until frothy and bubbly. Adjust sweetness if necessary.

5. **Assembly time:** Divide the tapioca pearls and syrup among 6 tall glasses. Pour in the honeydew milk tea. Decorate each glass with a large bubble tea straw. Stir well.

BLACK TAPIOCA PEARLS (*HỘT TRÂN CHÂU*) Make sure to look for black tapioca pearls, which can be found in any Asian specialty markets or online. American pearl tapioca won't work for this drink as it will fall apart and become a starchy mess. You must use tapioca pearls made just for bubble tea. Once cooked, store them in syrup, stirring periodically to prevent lumping, and use them the same day for optimum results.

HONEYDEW BUBBLE MILK TEA WITH TAPIOCA PEARLS:
Trà Sữa Dưa Honeydew Trân Châu

RED AZUKI BEAN DESSERT

Chè Đậu Đỏ Bánh Lọt

YIELDS 6 SERVINGS

> *Chè đậu đỏ bánh lọt* is a colorful dessert. Although in Western culture red beans (*đậu đỏ*) are used in savory dishes, in Asia they are primarily used for making sweets. This dessert is composed of five colorful layers: sweet red beans, split yellow mung beans (*đậu xanh*), green pandan-flavored (*lá dứa*) jelly noodles (*bánh lọt*), mock pomegranate seeds (*hột lựu*), and sweet coconut milk.

¾ cup dried azuki beans (*đậu đỏ*)

1½ cups rock sugar (*đường phèn*) (or granulated sugar), to taste

1 cup Chinese brown sugar (*đường thẻ*) (or regular brown sugar)

3 cups plus 2 quarts water, divided use

3 tablespoons split yellow mung beans

½ cup water chestnut flour (*bột củ năng*)

¼ teaspoon pandan extract (*mùi lá dứa*)

3 cups unsweetened coconut milk

¼ teaspoon jasmine extract (*nước hoa mùi hoa lài*) (optional)

Pinch salt

1 red beet, peeled and cut into quarters

2 cups fresh water chestnuts, peeled

1 cup tapioca starch

1 quart shaved ice

THE DAY BEFORE:

1. **Preparing the azuki beans:** Wash and rinse the azuki beans thoroughly in several water baths (about three times), discarding any floating or odd-shaped beans. Cover the beans completely and soak in cold water overnight.

THE NEXT DAY:

2. **For the syrup:** Place 1 cup each rock sugar and Chinese brown sugar in a saucepan. Add 3 cups water. Bring to a boil, then let simmer until the sugar is completely dissolved. Remove from the stove and cool to room temperature.

3. **Cooking the azuki beans:** Drain the beans. Fill a saucepan with 1 quart of the water and bring to a boil. Add the azuki beans and cook for about 1–2 hours until softened. Stir every now and then so the beans don't stick to the bottom of the saucepan. Check for doneness after 1 hour; the beans should be soft when gently pressed between your thumb and index finger. If not, add 1 cup water and cook for 30–60 minutes until softened. Turn off the heat, add ¾ of the syrup, and stir well. Cover and let sit for 30 minutes.

4. **For the mung beans:** Wash and rinse the mung beans thoroughly in several water baths (about three times). Discard any floating or odd-shaped beans. Drain, removing as much water as possible. No soaking time is required. Place the mung beans in a small saucepan and cover with 2½ cups water. Bring to a boil, then lower the heat to medium-low. Cook for 20–30 minutes, stirring occasionally, until the skins burst and the mixture thickens. The beans should be very soft, almost like a paste. Drain again; once they have dried, add the remaining syrup. Stir well.

5. **For the pandan jelly noodles:** In a nonstick saucepan, combine the chestnut flour, 2 tablespoons of the rock sugar (or granulated sugar), pandan extract, and ⅔ cup cold water. Whisk the mixture with a mini whisk or chopsticks. Cook over medium-low heat for 8–10 minutes until thickened; make sure to stop cooking the jelly noodle mixture as soon as it becomes thick (but not dry). When the mixture becomes almost like modeling clay, remove from the heat. Cover a flat surface with a sheet of parchment paper or plastic wrap. Sprinkle with a thin layer of chestnut flour and

transfer the jelly noodle mixture. Let cool. Flatten the mixture and place another sheet of parchment paper on top like a sandwich. Using a rolling pin, even out to about ¼" thick. Cut into ½" pieces using a crinkle-cut knife (you don't have to cut them with this specific vegetable carving knife, but it's the design traditionally used). Fill a saucepan with cold water and bring to a boil. Add the cut jelly noodles, bring back to a boil, and then immediately lower the heat to medium. Cook for 2–3 minutes, until the jelly noodles float to the surface. Using a slotted spoon, transfer them to an ice water bath to stop the cooking process; this will give them a chewy texture. Chill in the refrigerator in the ice water bath until you're ready to serve.

6. **Sweetening the coconut milk:** In a separate saucepan, combine the coconut milk and the remaining rock sugar (2–4 tablespoons). Bring to a boil; add jasmine extract (if using) and a pinch of salt. Adjust sweetness; it should be lightly sweetened. Let cool to room temperature.

7. **For the pink coloring:** Place the beet in a large saucepan and cover with cold water. Bring to a boil, then lower the heat to a gentle simmer. Cook for 10–15 minutes until softened. Remove the beet and reserve it for use in another dish, such as a salad. Cool the beet water to lukewarm. Note: For faster prep time, you could dye the water with red food coloring and sweeten it with a bit of sugar.

8. **For the mock pomegranate seeds:** Cut the water chestnuts into cubes the size of pomegranate seeds. Soak them in the lukewarm beet liquid for 5–10 minutes until the chestnuts turn into a pinkish color. Place tapioca starch in a deep plate and transfer the red-tinted water chestnuts to the plate. Toss the pieces until well coated. Remove the excess tapioca starch from the water chestnuts using a large mesh strainer. Fill a saucepan with cold water and bring to a boil. Add the water chestnuts one piece at a time to prevent them from sticking to each other (cook them in batches of about 2 dozen each). Bring the water back to a boil and then immediately lower the heat to medium. Cook the water chestnuts for 2–3 minutes, until they float to the surface. Using a slotted spoon, transfer them to an ice water bath to stop the cooking process and create a chewy texture. Chill in the refrigerator in the ice water bath until you're ready to serve.

9. **Assembly time:** Divide the red beans among 6 tall glasses. Top with a few teaspoons of mung beans. Using a slotted spoon, cover with a spoonful of green noodles and a few mock pomegranate seeds. Cover with shaved ice to the top of the glass and complete with sweetened coconut milk. Serve with a long-handled spoon and a straw.

MOCK POMEGRANATE SEEDS Fresh water chestnuts are used in this recipe, but you could use canned water chestnuts instead; use ½ (4-ounce) can. Another alternative is to use fresh jicama.

RED AZUKI BEAN DESSERT: *Chè Đậu Đỏ Bánh Lọt*

DURIAN SMOOTHIE

Sinh Tố Sâu Riêng

YIELDS 3 SERVINGS

If you've never tasted durian, you will either absolutely love it or find the taste and fragrance peculiar. In Asia, it is considered a delicacy. *Sinh Tố Sâu Riêng* has a creamy, succulent texture; the adventurous foodies in your life will appreciate this smoothie!

2 cups durian, seeded

2 cups ice cubes, crushed

¾ cup soymilk, as needed (depending on how you like the consistency of your shake)

3 tablespoons sweetened condensed milk, to taste

1 tablespoon honey (optional)

In a blender, combine all the ingredients until very smooth. Adjust the sweetness with honey (if using) and the consistency with more soymilk (if needed). Divide into 3 tall glasses.

HOW TO OPEN A DURIAN Durians are covered with spikes and can be very heavy, so handle with care. Before cutting the durian, make sure the work surface is covered with newspaper. (You may want to keep a sharp knife exclusively for this kind of fruit—the outer skin is very tough.) Make a long incision (about 10") starting from the stem. Dig your hands into the opening and use as much force as needed to open and pull the fruit apart. Scoop the durian pods out of the husk. Using the knife, score another incision in the center and you will find another section of durian pods. Repeat until all the pods are gathered.

SAPOTA FRUIT SHAKE

Sinh Tố Sapôchê

YIELDS 6 SERVINGS

In Asia, *sapôchê* is a popular fruit, especially on very hot days. Its juice has a great cooling effect. If you're lucky enough to find fresh sapota in your area, you have to give this a try. Otherwise, you could use canned sapota (sometimes also known as *chikoo*). Although the canned version isn't quite as flavorful, it will still make you fall in love with this drink.

5 sapotas

1 quart ice cubes, crushed

1½ cups soymilk, as needed (depending on how you like the consistency of your shake)

½ cup sweetened condensed milk, to taste

1 tablespoon honey (optional)

1. **Sapota preparation:** Peel the sapotas, discard the seeds, and coarsely chop.

2. **Assembly time:** In a blender, combine all the ingredients until very smooth. Adjust the sweetness with honey (if using) and the consistency with more soymilk (if needed). Divide into 6 glasses.

THAI BASIL SEED DRINK

Nước Hột É

YIELDS 12 SERVINGS

This odd-looking drink is, despite its appearance, very refreshing. Once soaked in warm water, the seeds form a kind of gooey-textured shell. In addition to the Thai basil seeds, soaked malva nut tree seeds are usually included in this unusual drink.

⅓ (2-ounce) package dried malva nut tree seeds (*đười ươi*)
¼ cup Thai basil seeds
2 quarts water
½ cup superfine sugar, to taste
4 tablespoons honey
3 cups ice cubes, or more
2 limes, freshly squeezed

1. **Preparing the malva nut tree seeds:** Cover the malva nut seeds completely in warm water and soak for 30 minutes. Separate the cotton-like texture from the skin and seeds, discard the skin, and rinse the cotton-like texture in cold water. Squeeze out as much liquid as possible using paper towels. Set the seeds aside.

2. **Preparing the Thai basil seeds:** Place the basil seeds in a large strainer and rinse them under running water. Place the rinsed seeds in a large heatproof pitcher.

3. **Assembly time:** In a saucepan, bring 2 cups of the water to a near boil. Pour into the pitcher. Let the basil seeds gain in volume, which will take about 5 minutes. In the same saucepan, dissolve the superfine sugar with 1 cup of the water. Bring to a near boil, then add the honey. Pour the resulting syrup into the pitcher. Add the remaining 5 cups of cold water and complete with lots of ice cubes. Add the lime juice and the malva nut tree seeds. Stir well. Adjust sweetness if necessary.

THAI BASIL SEED DRINK: *Nước Hột É*

VIETNAMESE COFFEE

Cà Phê Sữa

YIELDS 1 SERVING

Cups of Vietnamese coffee are individually brewed in a metal drip filter called *cà phê phin* using freshly ground, dark, extra bold roast blend coffee. To make this *cà phê sữa* authentic, sweetened condensed milk is added. This drink will give you plenty of energy and is a great way to wake up and keep going for the rest of the day.

1 cup filtered water
3 tablespoons dark roast coffee, freshly ground
1 Vietnamese coffee filter
3 tablespoons sweetened condensed milk, to taste

1. **Preparing the water:** Heat 1 cup of cold, fresh, filtered water (so there's no taste from the chlorine often present in regular water). Bring the water to a near boil (about 200°F).

2. **Making Vietnamese coffee:** Place the dark roast, freshly ground coffee in the Vietnamese coffee filter and add the top screen from the filter. Tighten the screw of the filter so that the coffee does not escape, then cover with the lid. Place condensed milk into the bottom of a (15-ounce) heat-proof glass, and place the glass underneath the coffee filter. Make sure the water is still hot, lift the lid, then pour in a little bit of water at a time until the filter is totally submerged and starts dripping. Fill the filter completely with water (make sure you don't pour too much so it doesn't overflow) and cover. It will take 5 minutes for the water to flow. It is the authentic method (small volume), but it's a very slow, low-tech utensil.

3. **Serving suggestion:** Serve the drink in the same tall glass with a long stemmed spoon and Deep-Fried Bread Sticks (*Bánh Giò Chéo Quẩy*) or Vietnamese Baguette (*Bánh Mì Baguette*) (see Chapter 1 for both recipes) on the side. Let the person who drinks the coffee stir the condensed milk into the coffee; there's something whimsical about the simple thrill of watching the coffee turn a caramel color.

VIETNAMESE ICED COFFEE   You're only one step away from turning *cà phê sữa nóng* (hot coffee) into *cà phê sữa đá* (iced coffee). Simply pour the hot coffee into a glass filled with cracked ice. Hot or cold, *cà phê sữa* is the perfect beverage for whatever season it is. Both are just as delicious. Note: For the iced coffee version, you could adjust the sweetened condensed milk quantity and also add cream (or half and half) to your own taste, even thought to *cà phê sữa* purists, the addition of cream and more sweetener might seem unnecessary.

GLOSSARY OF VIETNAMESE COOKING TERMS

You can find all ingredients listed here in most Asian/Vietnamese markets and most health food stores, unless stated otherwise. All ingredients are also available online.

Ăn: Eat

Bánh: Cake

Bánh cam: Literally translates to "orange-colored cake." Sweet, deep-fried sesame ball.

Bánh đa mè đen: Black sesame rice crackers

Bánh kẹp: Waffle. Literally translates to "tightly closed bread."

Bánh lọt: Jelly. Literally translates to "falling cake."

Bánh mì: Bread

Bánh patê sô: Literally translates to "hot pâté pastry."

Bánh phồng tôm: Vietnamese specialty shrimp chips ("*phồng*" means "puffed")

Bánh tiêu: Sesame sweet beignet

Bánh tráng: Dried rice paper sheets sometimes used for *chả giò* (in Southern Vietnamese version).

Bánh tráng mỏng: Literally translates to "thin paper sheets." They're usually made of tapioca and are used for wrapping *Gỏi cuốn.*

Bò: Beef

Bơ: Avocado, also means butter

Bột: Flour

Bột gạo nếp: Glutinous rice flour

Bột khai: Baking ammonia. Can be found online or in most Asian specialty markets. It will help make the bread light and airy. It has a very strong ammonia smell that disappears once it's cooked. If you want to substitute baking powder, I recommend you use Rumford brand aluminum-free baking powder. In general, Vietnamese cooking calls for single-action baking powder.

Bột năng: Tapioca starch

Bột nêm: Mushroom seasoning salt. Can be found in most Asian markets. Check out Korean markets too. Can be replaced with regular salt.

Bột ngô: Cornstarch

Bún: Vermicelli rice noodle

Cá: Fish

Cà chua: Tomato

Cá mòi: Sardine

Chả: Sausage-shaped patty

Chả giò: Eggroll

Chả lụa: Bologna sausage

Chiên: Fried

Cà pháo: Small round white eggplant

Cà phê: Coffee

Cà phê phin: Coffee filter. *Phin* is the pidgin French term for "filter." It can be found in most Asian specialty markets or online.

Cà rốt: Carrot

Cà tím: Eggplant

Cây xà lách: 1 bunch salad. It's the pidgin term for "salad" (*xà lách:* Vietnamese language swallows the consonant sounds from the French term). *Cây* is a quantifiable element and means "unit."

Chấm: Dipping

Chay: Vegetarian

Chè: Sweet, soupy, pudding-like dessert

Chim: Egg

Chim cút: Quail egg

Chua: Sour

Củ cải: Radish

Củ cải đường: Beet

Củ cải trắng: Daikon

Củ kiệu: White (root) onions from Asian green onions. They're pickled in brine and sold canned.

Củ năng: Water chestnuts. If you can't find the fresh version, you can use canned water chestnuts.

Củ sắn: Jicama

Cua biển: Crab

Đá (cà phê sữa đá): Literally translates to "stone," but in this case it means "icy cold"

Đậu: Bean

Dầu hào: Oyster sauce

Đậu ve: String beans

Đen: Black

Đinh hương: Clove

Đỏ: Red

Dừa: Coconut

Dưa mật: Cantaloupe

Dưa mật tây: Honeydew melon

Đu đủ: Papaya

Dưa: Pickled

Đường: Sugar

Đường mạch nha: Maltose

Đường phèn: Rock sugar

Đường thẻ: Chinese brown sugar

Gà: Chicken

Gạo: Rice

Gạo nếp: Glutinous, sticky rice, also known as sweet rice

Giá: Bean Sprout

Gỏi: Salad

Gỏi cuốn: Spring roll/summer roll/salad roll

Gừng: Ginger

Hẹ: Chinese chives

Hoa: Flower

Hoa lài: Jasmine

Hột: Grain

Khô: Dried

Kho: Braised

Khô Bò: Jerky

Lá: Leaf

Lá dứa: Padan

Lựu: Pomegranate

Măng: Bamboo

Măng tây: Asparagus

Mật ong: Honey

Mè: Sesame

Mì: Wheat

Mì căn: Literally translates to "stretched wheat"/wheat gluten, also known as Western seitan

Món: Dish

Món ăn chơi: Finger food/party food/appetizer

Mùi: Essence

Muối: Salt

Nấm: Mushroom

Nấm bào ngư: Abalone mushroom/King oyster mushroom

Nấm hương: Shiitake mushrooms

Nấm mèo: Wood ear mushroom. If you can't find the fresh version, you can use the dried version and rehydrate them in lukewarm water for 20 minutes before using them.

Nấu: To cook

Nem: "Spring roll"/sausage

Ngò gai: Cilantro, Vietnamese herb, literally translates to "thorny cilantro"

Ngò rí: Vietnamese Cilantro

Ngó sen: Lotus stem

Nóng: Hot

Nước: Water

Nước chấm chay: Vegetarian dipping sauce

Nước dừa: Coconut soda; can be found in any Asian market. You could also use coconut water or plain water.

Nước mắm chấm: Dipping sauce made with fish sauce

Ốp la: From the French *oeufs au plat*, meaning sunny-side up eggs.

Phèn chua: Potassium alum. It's sold in bulk form in 17.637-ounce packages in any Asian market.

Pho mát: Cheese

Rau huế: Thai basil

Rau răm: Vietnamese coriander

Rau thơm: Fragrant herb

Rượu nấu ăn: Cooking wine

Sapôchê: Sapote/sapota/sapodilla

Sầu riêng: Durian

Sen: Lotus

Sinh Tố: Vitamin/frappé drink

Sốt: Sauce

Sữa: Milk

Su hào: Green kohlrabi/Asian turnip

Sừng: Horn

Táo: Apple

Tàu hũ: Tofu

Tàu hũ ky: Tofu skin/Yuba. Can be found fresh in Asian market in the Bay Area (California) or frozen in most Asian specialty markets.

Tây: French

Tía tô: Perilla leaves (Vietnamese herb)

Tiêu: Hollow. Can also mean "black pepper" in reference to *hat tiên.*

Thì là: Dill

Thinh: Jasmine rice flour

Thịt ba chỉ: Pork belly

Thịt ba rọi: Fattiest part of the meat, similar to pancetta

Thịt nạc dăm: Tenderloin (lean part)

Tôm: Shrimp

Trà: Tea

Trái cây: Fruit

Trân châu: Pearl. Look for large, black tapioca pearls. If you can't find them, this ingredient can be omitted or replaced with homemade jelly noodles called *rau câu.*

Trứng: Egg

Xà lách: Salad, usually lettuce.

Xà lách son: Vietnamese watercress with unique flavor, similar to the French *mâche* salad

Xá xíu: Char siu

Xanh: Green

Xào: Stir fry

Xì dầu: see "*Xì dầu Maggi*"

Xì dầu Maggi: French brand of seasoning sauce, extremely popular in Vietnam. Can be found in most Vietnamese specialty shops. (Also known as Maggi Seasoning.)

Xoài: Mango

INDEX

W

X

ABOUT THE AUTHOR

JACQUELINE PHAM started PhamFatale.com to interact with other foodies who share her passion for gourmet cooking and international culture. Born in France to Vietnamese immigrants, Jackie developed an appreciation early on for both cuisines. On the weekends, her family would buy baguettes from the local *boulangerie* and Asian ingredients from *Tang Frères*, the famed *quartier chinois* (Chinatown) supermarket in the 13th *arrondissement* of Paris, so her family could make their own *bánh mì* sandwiches.

Since moving to the San Francisco Bay Area to be with her husband, Jackie has taken advantage of the easy access to quality Vietnamese ingredients and to her aunt who is an accomplished *restaurateur*. Many of the recipes she learned as a child and mastered as an adult appear in this book or on PhamFatale.com.

In addition to recipe development for her website and cookbooks, Jackie has experience developing, testing, and photographing dishes for food manufacturers. She also had the opportunity to cook for a Nobel laureate, several *Fortune* 100 executives, a former U.S. ambassador to the United Nations, and even a famous Hollywood actor! Visit *www.phamfatale.com/banh-mi* for more tips and videos to help you replicate the same dishes.